But I Didn't Say Goodbye

Helping Families After a Suicide

But I Didn't Say Goodbye

"What can I add to the chorus of praise for Barbara Rubel's *But I Didn't Say Goodbye?* Just this: that it rang true to me as a survivor of my own father's suicide at the same age as the fictional protagonist of her account, and that it passed muster with me as a researcher and clinician who both studies and accompanies survivors of similar loss. In a field that is too often characterized by arid academic treatises filled with theories and statistics on one hand, and impassioned but subjective personal accounts on the other, Rubel has produced something distinctive: an evidence-informed and contemporary treatment of a devastating form of loss that uses the artful device of a hypothetical case study to render it in human terms. I applaud this integrative vision and will recommend it frequently to other clinicians and trainees attempting to close the gap between theories of suicide bereavement and actual practice."

—Robert A. Neimeyer, PhD
Director of the Portland Institute for Loss and Transition, Editor of *Death Studies* and *New Techniques of Grief Therapy: Bereavement and Beyond*

"Barbara Rubel is a great teacher who has known and worked with many suicide loss survivors. She teaches not only what she has learned from them, but also what she has learned from her own experience as a survivor. Her method of teaching is as old as humanity—by telling a story. The story is about Alex, an 11-year-old boy who loses his dad to suicide. Through this story, Barbara helps the reader to understand what losing someone to suicide might be like for a child. Then she also adds the voice of that same boy when he is 21, reflecting back on how this loss has changed his life, wounding him, but also helping him to grow. And she also includes the voices of the adults in Alex's family (parent, uncle, and others) as they react to the loss.

In *But I Didn't Say Goodbye,* Barbara Rubel has combined our modern academic theories of grieving, and the research that supports those theories, and then translated them into a readable story for anyone bereaved by suicide. Packed with information and wisdom, readers will find their own journey as a survivor mirrored in the narrative of Alex. Reading *But I Didn't Say Goodbye* will help any individual or family—adults, adolescents, and children—who faces the loss of someone to suicide to better understand themselves and their family members who are grieving a similar loss."

—John R. Jordan, PhD
author of *Grief After Suicide: Understanding the Consequences and Caring for the Survivors* and *After Suicide Loss: Coping with Your Grief,* 2nd ed.

"There can't be enough praise for *But I Didn't Say Goodbye.* Everyone should read this book, whether you lost someone to suicide or not. The unique way in which *But I Didn't Say Goodbye* tells Alex's story; it brings you throughout his life and how surviving a tragedy can be reality—a message we need to share with other survivors so that they can have hope. For as hard as the topic is, you will be inspired in the end. Buy this, read it, and talk about it with the people in your life."

—Dan Reidenberg, PsyD
Executive Director of SAVE—Suicide Awareness Voices of Education

"Studying suicide is hard. Barbara Rubel doesn't make it easy, but she does take the student by the hand and leads them through the brambles—thorns and all—to a safe place of understanding on the other side, where tolerance, compassion and empathy become possible. No other book on this difficult topic is as well organized, documented, or user-friendly. If more students would read this book, our recruitment into this life-saving work would be much, much easier."

—Paul Quinnett, PhD
President and CEO, The QPR Institute, Inc.

"There are a lot of books out there about suicide and the impact such a death has on those who are left behind. Many of them, unfortunately, are too preachy, too judgmental, and/or too pat in delving into the myriad of actions and reactions people have when they're coping with the suicide death of a family member or friend. *But I Didn't Say Goodbye* is thoughtful and incorporates helpful information without falling into those traps. It's a good book for professionals as well as those who are coping with the loss of someone who took their own life. Thought provoking and packed with provocative information, Rubel's 3rd edition of this book will help those struggling to understand why someone dies of suicide, and how to support those left behind."

—Donna Schuurman, EdD, FT
Senior Director of Advocacy and Training/Executive Director Emeritus, The Dougy Center: The National Center for Grieving Children & Families

"Grief is letting go of a future you will not get to have, but if you can find meaning and purpose after the tragic loss of a loved one to suicide, it may not entirely take the pain away, but it may help you live *with* life never being the same again. Barbara Rubel's, *But I Didn't Say Goodbye,* is possibly the best guide and road map to making that happen."

—Mark Goulston, M.D.
co-creator and moderator: *Stay Alive: An Intimate Conversation About Suicide Prevention* and author of *Just Listen: Discover the Secret to Getting Through to Absolutely Anyone.*

"Barbara Rubel's *But I Didn't Say Goodbye* provides invaluable insights into the experiences of those who have lost a loved one to suicide. These insights derive from personal experience of the author as well as interactions helping many other survivors of suicide loss. Additionally, the book provides an informed overview of what is known about loss by suicide, not only from survivors' personal experiences, but also reflecting current research, theory, and writings on suicide loss survivors. The relaying of this information after the overview is provided in narrative form. Though focusing primarily on an 11-year-old son following his father's suicide, the story describes the many interactions and personal thoughts experienced by one family and its several members in the aftermath of a family member's suicide.

Practical and real-life information are embedded within this narrative that could serve as models and examples for family, clinicians, and others who experience suicide loss, or interact with or help suicide loss survivors. Included also are activities and questions to discuss and consider at each point of the grief and bereavement process. The narrative revisits the family members, not only during the immediate aftermath of their loss and the many thoughts, emotions, questions, and activities that occur at that time, but also in the early months after the death, as well as after a year, and finally ten years following the loss. The book can and should be read by adults (including professionals) as well as adolescents to help them following suicide loss."

—John L. McIntosh, PhD
co-author of *Suicide and Its Aftermath: Understanding and Counseling the Survivors* and *Grief After Suicide: Understanding the Consequences and Caring for the Survivors.* Professor Emeritus of Psychology, Indiana University South Bend

"A tremendous source of education and support for clinicians, survivors and all who support those bereaved by suicide. *But I Didn't Say Goodbye* is both comprehensive and concise, providing a unique perspective to coping with suicide loss developmentally through creative narrative."

—Jill Harrington-LaMorie, DSW, LCSW
Adjunct Faculty, The Chicago School of Professional Psychology/ Rutgers University, Grief Therapist, Research Consultant and author of *Surviving Families of Military Suicide Loss: Exploring Postvention Peer Support*

"The format of the chapters (immediate to the time, 10 years later, questions) was solid. In fact, the 10 years later piece could give people hope in the immediate aftermath. And the questions, which I often find to be superficial and not helpful, clearly come from a place of thoughtful consideration. I also loved the exercises and the fact that they're organized around a multifaceted perspective on grief."

—Kathleen R. Gilbert, PhD, FT
Professor Emerita, Indiana University-Bloomington School of Public Health

"After reading Barbara Rubel's book *But I Didn't Say Goodbye* I have deep regrets that this book was not available 60+ years ago when my father took his life when I was 10 years old. If I, and my family, had read this book, perhaps I would not have suffered so many years with magical thoughts that I might have saved him if I had been home that day, or my last memory of him would not have been in the open casket. What a great book for parents, children, grandparents, and friends to share and talk about after a suicide to help chart a course for growth after the trauma of a suicide. I highly recommend this book."

—Rabbi Daniel A. Roberts, DD, DMin, FT
co-author of *The Suicide Funeral (or Memorial Service):
Honoring their Memory, Comforting their Survivors*

"An important resource for all of us who have lost a loved one to suicide. Barbara Rubel extends a comforting hand and offers wise advice on a difficult subject and we are grateful for her help and support."

—Carla Fine
author of *No Time to Say Goodbye: Surviving the Suicide of a Loved One*

"*But I Didn't Say Goodbye* tells the story, from the perspective of a young son, of a family rocked by suicide and reeling from the aftermath. This book is a helpful guide for families who must face the emotional upheaval and the heartbreaking realities of their loss. It is not easy to walk the slippery path of shock and grief following a suicide. This practical and easy-to-absorb book is an excellent resource and will especially help families with young children."

—Adele Ryan McDowell, PhD
author of *Making Peace with Suicide:
A Book of Hope, Understanding and Comfort*

"Barbara Rubel has created an invaluable resource for families who are grieving the loss of a loved one to suicide. *But I Didn't Say Goodbye* is an impactful as it is absorbable, making it a realistic and tethering source of comfort for adults and children alike. Though the book's characters, Barbara brilliantly and organically captures the importance of adults helping kids grieve with honesty, patience, and compassion. Barbara carries the thread of grief beautifully throughout her work, reminding readers that one does not "get over" death; rather, one moves forward with it. I am grateful for the opportunity to share this book with children and families who, through reading it, will be reminded that they are not alone."

—Hallie Riggs, LCSW
Coordinator of The Den for Grieving Kids, Family Centers' Center for HOPE

"*But I Didn't Say Goodbye* is an invaluable resource for anyone who is caring for, or working with, bereaved children who are coping with the loss of someone close due to suicide. I have used this book extensively through the years and will continue to do so. *But I Didn't Say Goodbye* discusses the importance of being honest with children, especially when the cause of death is suicide. Withholding the truth doesn't help and causes children to feel isolated within their own families. The book also does a great job of explaining complex topics such as suicide, grief, and shame. Kudos to Barbara Rubel on the third edition of this important book."

—Pamela Gabbay, EdD, FT
author of *Understanding and Supporting Bereaved Children: A Practical Guide for Professionals*

"*But I Didn't Say Goodbye* just keeps getting better and better. This third edition has all the comfort of the second, plus more information and ideas. Good books should curl up on the couch with you and hold your hand. This one does that and more."

—Joy Johnson
Co-Founder, Centering Corporation

"But I Didn't Say Goodbye responds to Alex's questions of suicide, confident of promoting the child's healthy grief resolution and laying a sound foundation for the child's future well-being."

—LaRita Archibald
HEARTBEAT, Support in the Aftermath of Suicide

"The *But I Didn't Say Goodbye* comprehensive workbook discusses postvention truly is prevention for the next generation."

—Michelle-Linn-Gust, PhD
Survivor Division Chair, American Association of Suicidology, author of
Do They Have Bad Days in Heaven? Surviving the Suicide Loss of a Sibling

"Professionals, parents, and others can use this book as a foundation and guide to supporting survivors of suicide on their path towards healing."

—Ricky Greenwald, PsyD
Founder/Director, Child Trauma Institute, author of *Child Trauma Handbook*

"Barbara Rubel has written a much-needed fictional story that applies the thoughts, emotions, and experiences of a young boy who has lost his father to a suicide."

—Julia Sorensen
Therapist and author of *Overcoming Loss: Stories
and Activities to Help Children Transform Grief and Loss*

"But I Didn't Say Goodbye is an incredible resource written with compassion, empathy and insight."

—Doreen Cammarata MS, LMHC
author of *Someone I Love Died by Suicide:
A Story for Child Survivors and Those Who Care for Them*

"Barbara Rubel has given much of her professional life to the needs of the bereaved, especially those most marginalized."

—Rev. Richard B. Gilbert, PhD, CT
Faculty, Mercy College, Dobbs Ferry, NY

"SAVE applauds the honesty and accuracy of this book."

—Mary Kluener
President SAVE, Suicide Awareness Voice of Education

"I highly recommend this important resource."

—Virginia A. Simpson, Ph.D., FT
Founder, Executive Director & Program Director, The Mourning Star Center;
Director of Grief Education, FuneralOne

"I wish I'd had *But I Didn't Say Goodbye* when my brother Bill died by suicide 28 years ago . . . Use this book as a guide for your own healing the first time and as a source of solace every time thereafter."

—Mike Reynolds
author of *Survivor Bill*

"*But I Didn't Say Goodbye* serves as a practice resource and tool to work with children and adults with the delicate and sensitive topic of suicide."

—Linda Goldman
author of *Life and Loss, Breaking the Silence, Bart Speaks Out,
Raising Our Children to Be Resilient* and *Coming Out, Coming In*

"As someone who, as a child, lost his father to suicide, I warmly recommend Barbara Rubel's book."

—Larry Lockridge
Professor of English, NY University, author of *Shade of the Raintree:
The Life and Death of Ross Lockridge, Jr.,* author of *Raintree County*

THIRD EDITION

But I Didn't Say Goodbye

Helping Families After a Suicide

Barbara Rubel

Griefwork Center, Inc.
Kendall Park, New Jersey

Published in Kendall Park, New Jersey
by Griefwork Center, Inc.
P.O. Box 5177
Kendall Park, NJ 08824
www.griefworkcenter.com

ISBN: 978-1-892906-02-1
Library of Congress Control Number: 2019948488

Printed in the United States of America

This publication is designed to present information pertaining to the subject
matter covered. It is sold with the understanding that the author and publisher are not
providing psychological services. The author and Griefwork Center, Inc. have neither liability
nor responsibility to any individual with regard to any loss or harm caused, or alleged to be
caused directly or indirectly, by the material in this book. The fact that an individual, organization,
or website is referenced in this work as a citation and/or potential source of further information
does not mean that the author or the publisher endorses the information the individual,
organization, or website may provide or recommendations that it may make.

Limited Duplication License:
The publisher grants to individual purchasers of this book nonassignable permission
to reproduce materials in the appendix. This license does not grant the right to reproduce these
materials for resale, redistribution, electronic display, or any other purposes.

Permission:
To obtain permission for reprints and excerpts,
email: barbararubel@barbararubel.com

Contents

Acknowledgments 17

Foreword. 19

Preface 23

Introduction. 27

PART 1
How to Apply the Principles to the Story

What is Postvention 35

Suicide Loss Survivors 35

Grief After a Death by Suicide 37

When Grief Gets Complicated. 38

Factors that Influence Grief After a
Death by Suicide. 40

Helping Suicide Loss Survivors Cope
with Mourning 46

Bereaved Children 53

Postvention in the American Death System 57

When a Client Dies by Suicide. 59

PART 2
The Story

CHAPTER 1: The Worst Day. 67

CHAPTER 2: The Next Day 75

CHAPTER 3: Mourning 87

CHAPTER 4: Telling a Friend What Happened ... 97

CHAPTER 5: Keepsakes and Treasures 111

CHAPTER 6: A Bereaved Family.................... 121

CHAPTER 7: Positive Relationships 135

CHAPTER 8: A Children's Grief Support Center.. 145

CHAPTER 9: Three Months Later 155

CHAPTER 10: One Year Anniversary 165

APPENDIX A: Palette of Grief® 177

APPENDIX B: Guided Imagery for
Suicide Loss Survivors............................ 193

References.. 199

Resources.. 210

Additional Readings............................... 215

About the Author 219

ACKNOWLEDGMENTS

From the moment I decided to update and revise the third edition of *But I Didn't Say Goodbye* and throughout its multiple drafts, I have been encouraged by many talented people. They were helpful in integral ways: reading this work in manuscript form and offering helpful and constructive comments. I wish to thank everyone who provided input and feedback. There are several individuals who deserve to be singled out for their encouragement during this process: Cheri Andes, Lisa Athan, Heidi Bryan, Stacey Cohen, KC Delp, Michelle Doran, Serafina Georges, Karen Goldman, Brandy Lidbeck, Rachel Mehta, Penny Meyers, Dorothy Paugh, Sidney Pech, Janet Roberts, Diana Sebzda, and Tamara Starr. I am grateful to Dan Roberts who generously read my manuscript and provided spiritual insight. Thank you to the *Imagine* staff, a center for bereaved children where I took a tour and incorporated the design of their center into the story.

I am particularly grateful to Sherry Roberts and Debra Lefkowitz for their editorial comments and text editing. Debra edited the 4th edition of the Western Schools coursebook I authored, *Loss, Grief, and Bereavement: Helping Individuals Cope*. I consider myself fortunate that I was able to work with Debra again. I would also like to express my appreciation to Rebecca Finkel for her invaluable assistance in creating the cover design and formatting of this book. I want to especially acknowledge my family and close friends. I'm so glad we had this time together . . .

FOREWORD

In 1999, Barbara Rubel wrote her first edition of *But I Didn't Say Goodbye*. A decade later, a second edition came out. Now, twenty years later, do we really need a third edition?

Happily, the answer is a resounding "yes!"

There are two reasons for that strong affirmation. The first is that over the last decade our knowledge of suicide has grown exponentially. We know far more about sociology, psychology, and neuropsychology of suicide than we did a decade earlier. The field has changed. So has the book. This newest edition includes a Part I that discusses what we have learned about suicide and grief in a way that clinicians—new to the field and experienced—will find useful. There is another added piece as well. Alex, the eleven-year-old protagonist of the story, reflects on his initial perspectives a decade later.

This is not to even imply that prior editions of *But I Didn't Say Goodbye* should be tossed in the refuse. When the book came out 20+ years ago, it was a valued tool for clinicians who work with families to assist their children in understanding death by suicide. Barbara Rubel knows that well. She, after all, was not only a clinician but a suicide survivor.

So am I. I know the subtle effects that suicide can have over generations in a family. I only knew one of my grandparents—my maternal grandmother. I knew my paternal grandfather died in the early 40s of cancer—years before my birth. But the death of my maternal grandfather and paternal grandmother were shrouded in mystery. I later learned they both died by suicide.

When I found out—as a young adult—it seemed to tie some loose ends together. I was a mediocre student until my junior and senior years when the choice of Vietnam or college was starkly presented to my generation. I blossomed in college—making the dean's list from my first semester and graduating *summa cum laude.* Surprisingly, my dad's response to my achievements was a rather subdued "make sure you don't work too hard." Based on the frequent lectures of working to potential that I heard throughout school, it seemed a tepid response. The same comments continued in graduate school. After, I received my doctorate, my dad shared how proud he was of me. I gently reminded him that I never felt he appreciated my work throughout my studies. My dad then shared a horrific story.

A colleague of his had traveled to attend his son's college graduation. The son was not there to meet him as planned. When he went to his son's room, he found his son dead—hanging from a rafter. He could not face his father to tell him a failed course had prevented graduation. My dad then told me about our family's hidden history and the fears that were the inevitable inheritance of those deaths.

Even today, suicide can be stigmatized and disenfranchised. Survivors may be reluctant to share their stories—afraid that others will judge their families as dysfunctional and problematic.

One of the main reasons I like *But I Didn't Say Goodbye* so much is that it portrays a fully functional family coping with the aftermath of a suicidal death. That very premise is so reassuring to families. Moreover, it models real feelings and reactions and shows how even in the most difficult situations, families can still support one another. As a teacher, one of the first things I learned is that there is much more to be gleaned from positive models than the all too often negative narratives. It reinforces what Dr. Albert Cain, pioneer suicidologist, often said—"telling about suicide is a process not an event." We see that so well reflected in these pages.

In short, Ms. Rubel has rendered great service in this revision. *But I Didn't Say Goodbye* offers a rich review of the field, a compelling narrative of a boy's response to his dad's suicide, and an appendix full of resources. The book is truly a gift to clinicians, families, and most importantly, child survivors of suicide.

—Kenneth J. Doka, PhD

Professor Emeritus, The College of New Rochelle
Senior Consultant, The Hospice Foundation of America

PREFACE TO THE 2020 EDITION

Although the warm, bright sunlight was coming through my hospital window, it was the coldest and darkest day of my life. Having gone into early labor, I was in the hospital when I was told my dad had died by suicide. I was in shock and couldn't believe that he had taken his own life. My dad and I had been close. He had always been there for me, always accepting of me, always supportive and loving. He was an important part of my life—a part that I had taken for granted and assumed would always be there.

I was unable to attend my dad's funeral. Doctor's orders . . . complete bed rest. How could I not attend my father's funeral or be a part of the rituals after his death? I had no choice. I needed to remain in bed and consider the health of my unborn triplets. My mother told me that she was going to have the gravestone engraved with the words, "Loving Husband, Father, and Grandfather." Even though my father ended his life before the triplets were born, he would still be their grandfather.

When visitors arrived at my hospital room, they congratulated me on the birth of the triplets and in the same breath, told me how sorry they were about my dad's death. I didn't know how to feel. Was I supposed to be happy about being a new mom or sad because my dad had killed himself?

I was torn between the joy of having three healthy babies and the grief of knowing their grandfather would never hold them or know them, and they would never know him. Although it seemed so trivial, one of my biggest dilemmas was the placement of greeting cards I had received from family and friends. Should I mix the sympathy cards with those that congratulated me on the birth of my triplets or keep the cards separated on the hospital window shelf? Could I separate grief from joy when the emotions were so closely woven together?

I remember looking at the open door of my hospital room anticipating my dad's arrival. How could Dad not visit? How could he not see his three grandsons? Although I was kept busy caring for the triplets, there were frequent moments when thoughts of my dad's death would surface. My friends and family were supportive. They reassured me that my dad loved me, was proud of me, and was no longer in physical pain. Although they attempted to comfort me, the truth kept screaming at me: "*But I didn't say goodbye.*"

Because I had been in the hospital under complete bed rest in the weeks leading up to the triplet's births, I had not seen my father during the preceding month. I had no idea that my dad was thinking of killing himself. How could I possibly have known his intentions when I had not seen him? It didn't really matter; I still felt guilty. At the time, I knew nothing about suicide awareness. I realize now that I would not have even known what to look for. Yet, I felt guilty for not knowing that a man I loved and to whom I was so attached was thinking about ending his life.

I am often asked why I created the fictional characters of Alex and his family members for *But I Didn't Say Goodbye,* rather than writing about my father's suicide. The answer is simple. I have been inspired by the many individuals, from the very young to the very old, who are bereaved by suicide but chose to share their stories with me. As a thanatologist and speaker, I have met many suicide loss survivors, including clinicians who have lost a client to suicide, as well as individuals who have attempted suicide and lived. Elements of each person's story resonate with me.

Family connectedness has been shown to protect against suicide ideation and attempts among adolescents (Stone, Luo, Lippy, & McIntosh, 2015). For that reason, I stressed the connectedness Alex felt to everyone in his family, including his mother, Sherry; his five-year-old sister, Debbie; his Aunt Jillian and Uncle Alan; his grandparents; and his Uncle Sammy. Although each character's loss narrative sprang from my imagination, they are a compilation of the real stories that I have heard. The characters in this book were developed to provide the reader with an understanding of how to communicate effectively when faced with difficult questions and overwhelming feelings after a death by suicide.

INTRODUCTION

Twenty years have passed since the first edition of *But I Didn't Say Goodbye*, which has been praised for providing readers with insights into helping bereaved children and families after a suicide. Since the release of the second edition a decade ago, communities have continued to face a considerable number of deaths by suicide. This latest edition will guide the reader in understanding how a suicide can rock one's assumptive world, but also how it can awaken the person to occupy a position of strength, feel connected with others, and appreciate life. The information presented will help the reader understand the complexity of suicide and how a suicide loss survivor can struggle with making sense out of the death.

Traditionally, training in suicide prevention, intervention, and postvention is limited in the clinical curriculum. Most students in clinical programs graduate without a full best-practice educational curriculum. Competency-based training in suicide risk assessment and management is essential for all clinicians. Also important is an understanding of postvention.

But I Didn't Say Goodbye presents a story that illustrates the varying dynamics a suicide loss survivor experiences. This book is a guide that connects the intellectual understanding of suicide with the emotional outcomes. The narrator in the story is an eleven-year-old child named Alex. Through Alex's eyes, the reader will see the transformation of feelings after going through a major loss. Alex's story connects the principles of helping to a personal experience, which helps the reader understand the effects of suicide on a deeper level. Suicide is a unique psychological experience for the survivors. Clinicians, families, and suicide loss survivors must recognize the different ways in which people respond in suicide's aftermath, and know how to use the tools at hand to bring clients, family members, or themselves through the painful experience of loss.

How to Use This Book

This book is intended to be read from front to back. Although the reader may be tempted to jump around, the book is not meant to be read in that way and doing so will cause the reader to miss valuable information. The content and structure of the book have been carefully designed to sequentially address beliefs and attitudes about what causes individuals to take their life, the sorrow felt after a death by suicide, and how to find meaning in what happened.

Part 1 offers a basic understanding of postvention, suicide loss survivors, grief after a death by suicide, complicated grief, determinants of grief, mourning theories, bereaved children, the American death system, and clinician survivors.

The chapters in Part 2 build upon one another sequentially, from the day of the suicide to the anniversary of the death. At the end of each chapter, there are follow-up questions for adults to explore in counseling sessions, support groups, therapy sessions, or at home. These questions provide a road map and can be modified as needed.

Chapter 1: The Worst Day focuses on the emotional strain involved when adults tell a child that someone they loved has died of suicide. This chapter emphasizes the importance of being honest with children about the death and speaking to them in an age-appropriate manner.

Chapter 2: The Next Day identifies the concerns of bereaved families as they search for answers as to why someone died by suicide.

Chapter 3: Mourning illustrates the process of explaining mourning customs, rituals, and burial procedures to children prior to the funeral.

Chapter 4: Telling a Friend What Happened explores the difficulty of recounting the story for the first time and experiencing the natural back-and-forth movement between feeling intense grief and engaging in fun distracting activities.

Chapter 5: Keepsakes and Treasures focuses on how keeping personal possessions that once belonged to the deceased can help bereaved family members stay connected to the person who died.

Chapter 6: A Bereaved Family examines mourning rituals, ways to explain death to a child, fears that others in the family might die, and the comfort of religious beliefs and practices after a traumatic loss.

Chapter 7: Positive Relationships focuses on how teachers, coaches, friends, and relatives may fill the roles and jobs once performed by the deceased. It also discusses feeling shame, being worried about returning to school, and finding ways to say goodbye after a sudden death.

Chapter 8: A Children's Grief Support Center is a new chapter that presents the advantages of bereavement counseling for adults who are having difficulty managing their grief, and the benefits of a bereavement support group specifically for children.

Chapter 9: Three Months Later takes a closer look at how the grief process changes over time and the preoccupation with causality and responsibility as those bereaved by suicide regain a sense of order in their lives.

Chapter 10: One Year Anniversary reviews the lessons that have helped shape a family's experience one year after a suicide.

The chapters in this third edition have been substantially updated and clarified, based on personal experiences, mourning models, and the latest research. The suicide in the story is introduced through background information and memories of its eleven-year-old narrator, Alex, whose father Bill has died by suicide. To educate readers about a suicide loss survivor without exposing them to graphic depictions of a suicide, the method of suicide is not described. After a sudden and/or violent death, the bereaved know there was some level of suffering at the end of their loved one's life, which can intensify grief reactions (Armour, n.d.). Therefore, rather than focusing on the method of suicide, the story concentrates on the thoughts, feelings, and behaviors of the family members in suicide's wake.

Each chapter focuses on common concerns that families face after a death by suicide. The chapters provide a foundational understanding of the impact of suicide on children and adults, and offer information to support and prepare the reader to communicate effectively.

New to the third edition, each chapter ends with Alex reflecting 10 years later on his loss experience, introducing family members and friends in his recollections. The dialogue between a young child, adolescents, and adults in the story will show the reader how to develop honest, open communication among the traumatically bereaved.

Who Should Read This Book?

The third edition of *But I Didn't Say Goodbye* was revised specifically to provide guidance and education for clinicians (e.g., mental health providers, medical providers, social workers, psychologists, school counselors, and case managers) and families working together to help children and adults after a death by suicide.

However, this book is appropriate for anyone who has experienced a death by suicide, or wants to help someone who has gone through this tragic loss. Suicide is a public health problem; ethically, we all need to care about this challenge.

How to Apply the Principles to the Story

Typically, postvention extends over months during that critical first year, and it shares many of the characteristics of psychotherapy: talk, abreaction, interpretation, reassurance, direction, and even gentle confrontation. It provides an arena for the expression of guarded emotions, especially such negative affective states as anger, shame, and guilt.

—EDWIN SHNEIDMAN

What is Postvention?

According to Crosby, Ortega, and Melanson (2011), suicide is "death caused by self-directed injurious behavior with any intent to die as a result of the behavior" (p. 23). This book focuses on providing support to individuals who are struggling with the aftermath of a suicide. Postvention refers to the act of helping those affected by a suicide (Shneidman, 1969, 1972).

Whereas the goal of prevention is to stop people from becoming suicidal, and the goal of intervention is to reduce the likelihood of suicide by individuals who are deemed suicidal, postvention mitigates the harmful effects of suicide. The goal of postvention is to assist suicide loss survivors in recovering and avoiding harmful health outcomes after a death by suicide (Andriessen, 2009).

Postvention brings suicide prevention and intervention full circle by including all those who need support. Postvention for families, school systems, and communities helps individuals bereaved by suicide process their grief and decreases the likelihood of "imitative suicidal behavior" (World Health Organization, 2014, p. 37).

Suicide Loss Survivors

Despite a lack of empirical evidence, Edwin Shneidman in 1972 suggested that there were six suicide loss survivors for each suicide. A recent study posited that for every suicide, an estimated 135 people are exposed (Cerel, McIntosh, Neimeyer, Maple, & Marshall, 2014). Not necessarily bereaved because of the death, these individuals are nonetheless "forever changed by the suicide" (Cerel, Brown, Maple,

Singleton, Van De Venne, Moore, & Flaherty, 2019, p. 533). After a suicide, individuals who may feel the impact can be categorized as suicide exposed, suicide affected, suicide bereaved short term, or suicide bereaved long-term (Cerel, et al., 2014). These terms are defined as:

Suicide exposed individuals are people who either heard about or witnessed the suicide. They do not have to be connected by biological kinship. Suicide exposed individuals can include an acquaintance or coworker of the deceased, a subway conductor at the scene of the suicide, the funeral director, or a clergy member who supports the bereaved family. They usually have minimal reactions and do not need professional assistance.

Suicide affected individuals are also exposed to a suicide. This group might include a first responder, a neighbor, a teacher, or health professional. They may have only mild to ongoing reactions and might not need assistance to cope after a death by suicide.

Suicide bereaved short-term is a subset of the suicide affected individuals. The individuals in this subset were attached to the person who died. Short-term bereaved individuals can include a friend, a teacher, a coworker, or even the fan of a celebrity who died by suicide. Those who are suicide bereaved short-term adapt and move through grief over time.

Suicide bereaved long-term are a subset within the suicide bereaved short-term group. They are usually family members and very close friends of the deceased. They may feel "a high level of self-perceived psychological, physical, and/or social distress for a considerable length of time after exposure to the suicide of another person" (Jordan & McIntosh, 2011, p. 7). Those bereaved long-term may experience trauma symptoms or prolonged grief, which can last more than a year. They are at risk of suicide behavior and may need professional help to manage their painful loss.

Grief After a Death by Suicide

I use the term Palette of Grief® as a metaphor to describe the grief process after a death by suicide. A palette is the thin, flat, and usually oval board with a thumbhole used by artists to hold and blend their paint colors. Similarly, suicide loss survivors can apply a metaphoric palette to a domain of loss to hold and blend their grief. The Palette of Grief includes blending reactions that bereaved individuals see as colors of loss. This metaphor captures the grief process, which is a blending of physical, emotional, cognitive, behavioral, and spiritual reactions after a suicide. The Palette of Grief is further described in Appendix A. Clinicians are encouraged to copy, print, or download this handout. To make the activity easy to use, it is accompanied by concisely written instructions.

Generally, those bereaved by suicide and drug/alcohol-related deaths are more likely to become impaired than those bereaved by an accident, homicide, or natural death because of the stigma. Although depression is a clinical illness that requires treatment, bereavement is a normal process that does not need to be treated unless the feelings overwhelm the bereaved to a clinical degree. Suicide loss survivors may react with shock, guilt, relief, helplessness, and shame. They may experience social stigma, feel compelled to search for explanations or meaning, and be at increased risk for suicidal behavior.

When a relative dies by suicide, the bereaved have an increased risk for depression, admission to psychiatric care, and even suicide death (Pitman, Osborn, King, & Erlangsen, 2014). Those bereaved by suicide may experience a distorted sense of responsibility, feeling that they are being blamed for the death, and elevated feelings of anger directed at their loved one (Cerel, Padgett, Conwell, & Reed, 2009; Jordan, 2001). Furthermore, grief reactions after a sudden and/ or violent death include insomnia, anxiety, avoidance of reminders, and fear (Rheingold & Williams, 2018).

A bereaved person may think that they are feeling better until a trigger (e.g., the deceased loved one's birthday or anniversary of death, or seeing the place where the person died) causes strong feelings to resurface. When triggered, the grieving person may experience physical reactions such as sweating, crying, or shortness of breath.

Individuals who are bereaved after a death by suicide may repeatedly focus on the reasons for the death and its effects and ask if they could have done something to prevent the death (Eisma & Stroebe, 2017).

The response of family members in the story are typical of the reactions of individuals bereaved after a suicide. For example, Alex's mother Sherry ruminates and experiences severe grief reactions. Delespaux and Zech (2015) reported a strong association between rumination and the severity of grief. Rumination makes coping difficult. Although suicide is difficult to comprehend and grief can become complicated, most of the reactions depicted in the story are a normal part of bereavement after a suicide.

Appendix B is a visualization for you to use or to use with bereaved clients. Guided imagery can quiet the mind and the body. It is a tool to manage grief and allows for introspective exploration after a suicide.

When Grief Gets Complicated

The grieving process is one of the rare occurrences in which painful, intense emotions are broadly considered normal and appropriate (Scharer & Hibberd, 2019). Maciejewski and Prigerson (2017) maintain that clinicians should not pathologize normal bereavement. In 1997, Horowitz and colleagues created the first diagnostic criteria that included separation distress as an essential criterion for complicated grief. People with complicated grief consistently experience intense grief, regardless of the mode of their loved one's death (Tal et al., 2017). However, most people are resilient and even a majority of those who experience complicated grief do not need professional help. They are able to manage their separation distress.

In 2001, Prigerson and Jacobs modified the grief criteria, and called it prolonged grief. Ten years later, Shear and colleagues (2011) established new diagnostic criteria for complicated grief disorder and called it prolonged grief disorder (PGD), which met the standards of research for inclusion in the Diagnostic and Statistical Manual of Mental Disorders (DSM-5). The DSM-5 includes unexamined elements of complicated grief disorder in its expanded criteria for PGD and renamed it persistent complex bereavement disorder (PCBD) (Maciejewski & Prigerson, 2017).

According to Doka (2017), PCBD is a candidate disorder listed in the DSM-5 Appendix under "Disorders Requiring Further Study." The DSM-5 acknowledges that the body of evidence suggests a form of disorder, but states that evidence is insufficient to fully stipulate features of the disorder. PCBD is also included under "Emerging Measures and Models" in the DSM-5 and classified as an "Other Specified Trauma- and Stressor-Related Disorder" (Boelen & Smid, 2017).

For a diagnosis of PCBD, a minimum of one year must have elapsed since the death, and grief must be significantly distressful to a clinically extreme degree on most days. Symptoms include yearning, sorrow, preoccupation with the death, avoiding reminders, and feeling that life is empty. PCBD can occur with other conditions, such as major depressive disorder or posttraumatic stress disorder (PTSD) (Fleming & Drake, 2018). According to Lee (2015), no instrument has been designed specifically to measure PCBD symptoms; instead, researchers have used Prigerson and Maciejewski's "Inventory of Complicated Grief," an assessment tool tied to DSM-5 criteria.

Complicated grief is termed prolonged grief disorder in the *International Classification of Diseases (ICD-11)*, a global system of diagnosis for disorders. The *ICD-11* criteria for prolonged grief disorder are similar to the criteria for PCBD, except that at least six months must have passed since the death and the symptoms must impair social, occupational, or other important areas of functioning to a clinically significant degree.

Factors That Influence Grief After a Death by Suicide

Death-related factors, relationship issues, mental health and well-being factors, and socioeconomic circumstances are addressed throughout the book. Determinants of grief are the myriad factors that can affect reactions to a death by suicide and intensify the grief process (Worden, 2018). These factors include:

- manner of death
- unnatural death
- violent death
- preventable death
- sudden death
- unexpected death
- absence of anticipatory grief
- untimeliness
- traumatic death
- childhood trauma
- finding the body
- psychological proximity
- age of the deceased
- age of the bereft

- attachment styles
- stability
- concurrent stressors
- secondary losses
- economic problems
- culture
- ethnicity
- religion
- spirituality
- disenfranchised grief
- place of death
- coping responses
- grief styles
- past losses
- preexisting trauma
- psychiatric issues

Suicide is classified as an unnatural manner of death. It is considered a death that is sudden, unexpected, and often violent, which gives the bereaved no time to prepare for the loss. Under different circumstances, when families realize that their loved one is going to die, they have time to prepare and experience anticipatory grief (Spatuzzi et al., 2017). The family in *But I Didn't Say Goodbye* had no time to emotionally prepare due to the abrupt nature of the death. Alex's father Bill killed himself right before Alex's school play. The determinant of grief—untimeliness—is a factor that affects Alex's reactions and intensifies his grief process.

Suicide is a traumatic loss for children and adults. Alex experiences a childhood trauma that will remain with him throughout his lifetime.

Coping is an ever-changing effort to manage each loss that comes after his father's suicide. The family members in the story are cognitively processing the suicide because each of them is affected in their own way.

According to the National Action Alliance for Suicide Prevention (2015), those bereaved by suicide can be affected by psychological trauma, direct exposure, and imagined exposure.

Psychological trauma occurs when the bereaved reconstruct and think about the pain their loved one experienced. Complicated by the psychological force needed to die by suicide.

Direct exposure is when the bereaved witness what happened, discover the body, or see things related to the death scene, such as an autopsy report.

Imagined exposure occurs when, lacking direct exposure, the bereaved create "a mental image of what the dying process was like and what the deceased suffered as they died" (NAASP pg. 15). The characters in the story envision the death scene through their own mental images. Although no one was physically present when the death by suicide occurred, Sherry was home at the time and found her husband's body. Also, the mechanism and severity of injury are not identified. The aim is to focus not on how Bill killed himself, but on how the family is affected and copes with the loss as individuals and as a unit.

Psychological proximity is a potential mediating factor that focuses on attachment. It reflects each family member's relationship, kinship, and bond with the deceased. The quality of their relationship, how close or distant they were, and how dependent they were on each other affect the grief process. The family in the story was attached to Bill. Their individual loss narratives show that their close bond with him has not been broken because of his death.

At the time of the death, Alex was an adolescent and his father was middle-aged. These factors will influence how Alex grieves. Although Alex had loving parents and formed a secure attachment with his father, the severing of the physical bond is a traumatic experience. Fifty years ago, Bowlby and Parkes (Bowlby, 1980; Bowlby & Parkes, 1970) developed the attachment theory. This theory posits that attachment styles develop in response to the way in which infants and children bond with their parents or caregivers.

Alex's life is stable. He feels secure because the adults in his life are reliable and dependable, even though they are grieving. Alex's mother, Sherry, openly shares her feelings of loss with him. Alex learns from his mother how hard it is to talk about suicide and is influenced by the way she grieves. Although his life is stable, he is managing a concurrent stressor; his mother's intense grief. Alex sees her tears and recognizes the pain she is going through. Sherry struggles with the love she has for her husband and the anger she feels toward him because he killed himself. As Alex sees Sherry express conflicting emotions regarding his dad's suicide, he has a better understanding of and acceptance of his conflicting emotions.

Positive parenting is a protective factor against a parentally bereaved child's future mental health problems (Flahault, Dolbeault, Sankey, & Fasse, 2018). Sherry is doing what she can to help her children manage their father's death. A spouse may feel deserted and abandoned by their loved one, which causes an emotional conflict between being sad and being angry about the intentional act of suicide (Pitman, Osborn, King, & Erlangsen, 2014). Flahault, et al., (2018) found that bereaved children identify with, and compare their own grief to that of, their surviving parent and are influenced by how that parent grieves. For this reason, clinicians should also focus on the bereaved parent's grief to better help bereaved children.

Alex experiences secondary losses as he faces changes in his daily routine and losses in his assumptive world. He had always assumed his father would be there for him. Alex overhears his mother talking about finances and worries that his family might have to move if they can no longer afford to live in their home. Such economic problems might have become a secondary loss if Sherry had to sell their home and Alex had to change schools, but this was not the case. Thurman, Taylor, Luckett, Spyrelis & Nice (2018) found that after a parent's death, the surviving parent's grief level and new financial issues were related to an increase in complicated grief in adolescents.

Culture and religion are major influencing factors after a death. As a multi-cultural society, it is important to recognize individual beliefs and customs. Alex's family relies on a shared set of beliefs, practices, traditions, and customs that structure their behaviors and affect the way they mourn and express grief. Braam (2017) notes that the purpose of spirituality and religion is to present an outlook of "hope, relief, coping, or meaning in life" (p. 580). Alex is a suicide-bereaved adolescent who believes that his father is in heaven. He has after-death communication with his father. According to Hagström (2019), after-death communication (e.g., sense loved one's presence, hearing a voice, smelling a fragrance) should be normalized and supported in grieving adolescents. Acknowledging and sharing family customs also provides comfort.

Doka (2002) maintains that when family members do not feel socially supported or cannot openly acknowledge their loss or publicly mourn, they will experience disenfranchised grief. Survivors of sudden and/or violent loss (e.g., suicide, murder, drunk driving) can experience disenfranchised grief if they isolate themselves or have negative exchanges with others in their social network (Rheingold & Williams, 2018). Perceived lack of social support is a determinant of grief. Fortunately, the social exchanges among the adults and children in our story are positive. Neither Alex nor Debbie are unrecognized grievers. In fact, Sherry includes her children in the funeral planning. Although Alex does not experience disenfranchised grief upon returning to school, we gain insight into what that experience could be like for a bereaved child.

Alex's friend, Brian, tells Alex that his cousin died by suicide. This shows Alex that other children are also bereaved by suicide. Brian shares with Alex how he finds meaning in his cousin's life by reestablishing who his cousin was as a person—not just a person who died by suicide. Bottomley and colleagues (2019) maintain that this destigmatization of the deceased is an attempt to restore their personhood and reverse any disgrace associated with the act of taking one's life. Because the stigma of suicide prevents suicide loss survivors from getting help and increases grief difficulties, it is critical to reduce stigma.

According to Martin & Doka (2000) there are two patterns of grief expression—intuitive and instrumental. The patterns in Alex's family include intuitive and instrumental, but also a blended grieving style. Sherry is an intuitive-style griever who expresses her emotions. Feelings are intensely experienced with prolonged periods of con-fusion, inability to concentrate, disorganization, physical exhaustion, and anxiety. All of these are perfectly normal so soon after a death.

In contrast, Aunt Jillian adopts an instrumental style of grief. In this pattern, thinking predominates over feelings and feelings are less intense (Martin & Doka, 2000). Aunt Jillian is generally reluctant to talk about her feelings; control of herself and her environment are most important to her. Problem solving becomes a strategy for mas-tering her feelings, and emotions are more likely to be expressed in private than in public.

Other determinants of grief to consider include past losses, pre-existing trauma, and psychiatric issues.

Helping Suicide Loss Survivors Cope with Mourning

No single approach exists for applying bereavement support after a death by suicide, and most suicide loss survivors depend upon their support systems. As they struggle in suicide's aftermath, suicide loss survivors could benefit from understanding contemporary mourning theories. Many years ago, Kübler-Ross (1969) created a theoretical model for people who are terminally ill. Its five stages (denial, anger, bargaining, depression, and acceptance) were never empirically proven.

Kübler-Ross worked with terminally ill patients, not with individuals who were bereaved. Bereaved individuals do not go through five stages in processing grief. Although denial, anger, depression, bargaining, and acceptance are grief reactions, they are not stages experienced by suicide loss survivors.

But I Didn't Say Goodbye focuses on six mourning theories that propose ways for the bereaved to cope with mourning. These theories are: the six "R" processes of mourning (Rando, 1993); dual-process model of coping with bereavement (Stroebe & Schut, 2010); posttraumatic growth model (Tedeschi & Calhoun, 2004, 2012); meaning reconstruction (Neimeyer, 2001); four tasks of mourning (Worden, 2018); and continuing bonds theory (Klass & Steffen, 2018).

In Part 2 of this book, the reader will observe how the principles underlying these theories enable the story's characters to manage their loss. More in-depth presentation of these theories can be found in journals such as *OMEGA—Journal of Death and Dying, Death Studies,* and *Suicide and Life-Threatening Behavior.*

Six "R" Processes

Rando's (1993) process-based theory emphasizes six processes that move a bereaved individual through grief. Each character in the story *recognizes, reacts, recollects, reexperiences, relinquishes old attachments,* and *reinvests* their grief. The family moves in a linear fashion through six processes, which are grouped into three phases: *avoidance, confrontation,* and *accommodation.*

In the *avoidance phase*, mourners *recognize* that their loved one has died by suicide and is truly gone. In this phase, mourners acknowledge that their loved one is dead.

In the *confrontation phase*, mourners *react.* They feel the pain stemming from physical separation and the secondary losses associated with that separation. As the mourners focus on remembering their loved one, they *recollect* and *reexperience.* They recall good and bad memories, and gradually *relinquish* the attachment they once had to the deceased.

In the *accommodation phase*, mourners attempt to find meaning in the suicide by readjusting to their new normal. This can include taking on new roles. They reinvest their grief and redirect emotional energy into something that is important to them (Rando, 1993). For example, Aunt Jillian reinvested her grief by learning a gatekeeper training called Question, Persuade, Refer (QPR). Gatekeepers are members of a community who are trained in suicide awareness.

Four Tasks of Mourning

Worden's four tasks of mourning theory is a cognitive behavioral approach with specific goal-oriented tasks that help the bereaved cope with their loss.

To *accept the reality of the loss*, the family members in the story, including the children, attend the funeral. Alex openly displays personal belongings such as his father's baseball cap. He becomes aware of what he has lost, grows from that experience, and finds meaning in his father's life. In contrast, Alex's Uncle Sammy puts photos of his brother in a box and chooses not to view them. These characters accept the reality of the loss in different ways.

The family members also *process the pain of grief.* They share many complex emotional reactions. It takes Uncle Sammy several months to reconcile his loss and return to the restaurant where he and his brother always ate. Family members attempt to *adjust to a world without the deceased.* Sherry takes on roles previously performed by her husband, and Alex's coach, Andy, takes him to his practices and games. The family attempts *to find an enduring connection with the deceased in the midst of embarking on a new life.* Alex forms a new and different relationship with his coach. He does not feel disloyal to his dad, but instead keeps a connection to him at the games.

The family in the story must complete certain tasks to accept Bill's death. They process the painful feelings associated with his having taken his own life. They adjust and get accustomed to what happened, yet they maintain a spiritual connection with him.

Alex is accomplishing Worden's four tasks as he slowly *accepts the reality that his father has died.* He will process his grief at each stage of his development and will adjust to a world without his father. Alex will find an enduring connection with his father despite growing up without his father's physical presence.

The Dual-Process Model

The dual-process model explores how individuals move toward and away from coping with mourning (Stroebe & Schut, 2010). To reengage with life, suicide loss survivors must go back into the world despite being bereaved, and cope by oscillating back and forth with two types of stressors: loss-oriented (LO) behaviors (e.g., break bonds, deny the suicide occurred, and avoid grief); and restoration-oriented (RO) behaviors (e.g., try new activities, new roles, new relationships, and tasks of daily living).

Think of the oscillation as a heavy pendulum that swings back and forth. By controlling the force with which the pendulum oscillates, the suicide loss survivor can focus on ways to cope with grief, adapt to grief, and rest from grief (Cantwell-Bartel, 2018). In a study by Blackburn & Bulsara (2018), the bereaved oscillated between exhibiting LO behaviors, in which they attempted to make meaning of the death and continue the bonds with the deceased, and RO behaviors, in which they carry out the tasks that the deceased used to perform, such as overseeing the family finances.

The family in the story oscillates between the loss and restoration stressors. Alex does not experience high levels of distress because he does not use one type of coping disproportionately over the other. At times, he moves toward his grief as he cries over his father's death, yearns for him, and attempts to find meaning of the suicide.

At other times, Alex manages the various changes in his routine and does things his father used to do, such as flipping the switch on the fuse box. Bereaved individuals can become overwhelmed by their grief if they do not alternate between confronting their grief and engaging in restorative work (McManus, Walter, & Claridge, 2018). For this reason, Alex oscillates between a loss-oriented approach and a restoration-oriented approach.

Alex moves toward coping with mourning when he talks about his father's death by suicide with his friend, Brian. Then he moves away from coping with mourning as he distracts himself from grief by playing with Brian's hamster. Although not effortless, such movement allows Alex to rest from grief in a restorative way and he will move toward or away from his grief throughout his lifetime.

As time passes, the way Alex shares the story of his father's death will change. He needn't tell his story in the same exact way each time. Rather, he can explore ways to change it and find meaning in it as he manages both types of stressors in life.

Posttraumatic Growth Model

Tedeschi & Calhoun's posttraumatic growth model (2004) explores how some traumatically bereaved experience positive psychological change after having struggled with a highly challenging situation. Posttraumatic growth refers to being transformed in a positive way as the result of a traumatic experience that disrupts a person's assumptive world (Tedeschi & Calhoun, 2012). Those who are not resilient experience a change in their sense of self and they see themselves as being stronger or feeling closer to others because of the traumatic event. The five domains of PTG are:

1. greater strength,
2. closer relationships,
3. new opportunities or possibilities,
4. gratitude for life, and
5. intensifying spiritual life (University of North Carolina at Charlotte, n.d.).

Although less resilient people can experience posttraumatic growth, those who are more resilient can experience personal growth. The two are not the same. According to Lumb, Beaudry, & Blanchard (2017), a loss is not a requirement for growth, and only people who are less resilient experience posttraumatic growth after a loved one's death.

Continuing Bonds

According to Klass, Silverman, & Nickman's continuing bonds model (1996), mourners do not have to sever the bonds and can maintain an inner representation of the deceased to hold in their memories. Continuing bonds is a common feature of bereavement in almost all grief models and has been integrated into many professional bereavement care practices (Klass & Steffen, 2018).

Bereaved individuals continue bonds spiritually by including the deceased in their daily life, writing letters to the deceased, or creating a ritual that includes the deceased in some way (Williams & Rheingold, 2018). Alex and his family continue their bonds with the deceased and maintain a spiritual connection with him. Andriessen and colleagues (2018) found that grieving adolescents who continue the bonds with deceased loved ones in a positive and meaningful way manage their grief as they move on in life while honoring the life of the person who died.

Adolescents who had distressing experiences with the deceased reported feeling ambivalent about continuing bonds. Therefore, continuing bonds is not appropriate for all bereaved individuals. The bereaved family in the story continue their bond with the deceased in a positive way. Sherry tries to help her children maintain an attachment to their father, continue the bond they shared with him, and rely on their religious beliefs to manage a new world in which their father is absent.

Alex's coach, Andy, assumes some of the tasks that Alex's father used to perform. Because Alex's father always took him to his baseball games and team practices, Alex now has to relearn his world, in which his coach takes on that role. According to Attig (2001), relearning entails having to learn again how to be who you are in the world without a loved one by your side. Alex has to relearn how to live as a bereaved child in a world that has been forever changed by the act of suicide. Alex relearns his world whenever someone does something for him that his father used to do, or whenever he completes the task himself. Another way he relearns his world is by letting go of the physical bond that he shared with his father and creating a spiritual bond that he will carry with him into adulthood.

Meaning Reconstruction Model

The underpinnings of Alex's assumptive and relational world tremble after his father's death. As Neimeyer (2019) notes, the loss of a loved one can lead to anguished attempts to find meaning in the death and meaning in their own life. Alex's understanding of loss, ability to make meaning of the death, and reliance on his strengths, exemplifies how adolescents cope with a death by suicide relative to how their surviving parent is coping.

According to Neimeyer's meaning reconstruction model, the bereaved revise basic assumptions about their world. Under this social constructionist or narrative-focused model, mourners interpret the loss and create stories to reconstruct the meaning of their loss. These loss narratives allow the bereaved to incorporate the loss into their overall life story.

Bartel (2019) found that the grieving process may entail family members deliberately grieving together or choosing to grieve separately; each family has a different grief style and finds meaning by incorporating rituals and remembrances. The children and adults in the story share their loss in their own way, individually and together, as they attempt to find meaning in what happened.

In helping suicide loss survivors find meaning in their loss, the listener must make sure that they slow down as they listen, take their time, and not rush the conversation. What they experienced is intense. Exploring the story is painful and it takes time to make meaning out of what happened.

"When people tell stories about their loss, they link the meanings to make a coherent narrative" (Kawashima & Kawano, 2016, p. 371). In his landmark book, Viktor Frankl (1984) contends that individuals who experienced suffering are motivated to finding meaning and purpose in life. Although Alex and his family are devastated by Bill's death and experience anger, abandonment, stigma, shame, guilt, and rejection, their story embraces this sense of hopefulness and meaning-making.

Pritchard & Buckle (2018) maintain that the struggle to reconstruct meaning is greater for those bereaved by suicide. Although Alex and his family struggle to reconstruct meaning, they understand the goals that guide them; build their resilience; adapt to their loss; and experience both personal and relational transformation and growth.

Neimeyer, Cerel, & Maple (2017) maintain that active engagement in suicide-related research, peer support groups, and community activities helps suicide loss survivors in their coping process.

Bereaved Children

Alex's loss narrative reflects the intense emotional, cognitive, behavioral, physical, and spiritual grief reactions which are common after a death by suicide.

- **Emotional:** anxiety, mistrust, bitterness, inability to accept that his father is dead, embarrassment, self-blame that he did not prevent the death, stigma, fear of being left alone, longing for what used to be, and feeling unsafe as the result of a perceived lack of control.

- **Cognitive:** confusion caused by the sudden nature of his father's death, lack of opportunity to prepare or say goodbye, inability to concentrate, and thoughts that generate fear.

- **Behavioral:** disruptive actions, episodes of acting out impulsively, outbursts of aggressive behavior, silence about the death, avoidance of reminders of his father, excessive crying at certain times, sleep disturbances, and night terrors.

- **Physical:** stomachaches, headaches, chest pain, insomnia, exhausted, dry mouth, hives, nausea, sighing, and neck pain.

- **Spiritual:** anger at God, questioning why God let the death happen, and a belief that God does not care about him.

Postvention must focus on children as well as on adults. A child younger than 2 years of age benefits from predictable routines, reassurance, attention, and the affection of adults. Photos of the deceased, newspaper clippings regarding the death, obituary listings, and sympathy cards should be preserved as keepsakes for the child. A child who is 2 to 3 years of age benefits from finger painting, drawing, playing with blocks, singing songs and rhymes that help express his or her feelings, and receiving explanations of death in simple terms.

There are two children in the story: Debbie, a five-year-old, and Alex, her eleven-year-old brother. A child 3 to 5 years of age benefits from sharing feelings through sand, water, props, made-up stories with dolls, puppets, and play phones; drawing pictures of family members (alive and deceased); engaging in imaginary play, including wearing clothing and adult shoes to play a grown-up role.

Debbie is given short and honest answers to her questions and her "why?" questions are answered, no matter how many times she asks. Her mother, Sherry, provides explanations of death in physical terms (e.g., the heart stopped beating). Children in this age group benefit from being read picture-book stories which focus on understanding loss. They also benefit from maintaining established, secure routines, such as keeping a nightlight on to reduce fear of the dark.

A child 5 to 7 years of age benefits from interacting with adults who are able to answer difficult, repetitive questions in age-appropriate language, provide clear explanations of what happened, and respond without clichés or expressions that may confuse the child. Sherry explains why Debbie is sucking her thumb and needs to sleep with her. Adults need to recognize that a child may adopt old behaviors and should be allowed to regress.

If children in this age group start to test and act out, they need routines and discipline, inclusion in cultural bereavement rituals, extra time with a close adult to feel safe, discussion about their fears, and playtime with their friends. They can also create a memory box (e.g., painted shoebox) to store keepsakes and reminders of the deceased person.

A child 7 to 9 years of age benefits from adults who are sensitive to a child experiencing guilt and shame, and who offer honest answers to all questions. Children benefit from participating in solo and team games, group projects, puzzles, painting and drawing, outdoor play, and sports. Children who are offered choices will feel more in control. Lastly, adults should clearly explain cultural rituals to children in this age group and include them in those rituals.

A child 9 to 10 years of age benefits from support within the school curriculum. Lytje (2017) found that children and adolescents ages 9 to 17 feared being considered different from other students, and although they wanted to talk about their loss, they felt ambivalent as they pretended that "they were okay and as if nothing had happened" (pg. 293). Alex shares his fears of being ostracized from his classmates when he returns to school and, accordingly, does not want to talk about his father's suicide.

Adolescents, like Alex, can benefit from having a good role model; having rules in place; being given choices on how to be involved in mourning rituals; creatively expressing grief through music and poetry; maintaining a connection with the deceased through a linking item; having teachers who offer assistance and who are flexible with school work; and having open lines of communication and accurate information about what happened. They also can benefit from attending a same-age bereavement support group for direct hands-on care and support to help create bonds with other children who are going through similar situations and feelings.

Over a span of 7 years, Feigelman, Rosen, Joiner, Silva, & Mueller (2017) tracked young adults ages 18 to 26 who, as adolescents, had experienced the death of their parent(s) and found that the depression, illegal activity, drug use, suicidal thoughts and behaviors, and reduced self-esteem they experienced or engaged in as adolescents faded as they entered young adulthood. These findings suggest that bereaved adolescents are resilient and adapt over time.

In a separate study, 79% of the adults who had experienced the death of a parent at a young age reported that having gratitude and appreciating life increased their adjustment after the traumatic loss (Greene & McGovern, 2017). McNiel & Gabbay (2018) maintain that a child will adapt and integrate the loss into his or her life narrative. This contention is reflected in our story. Ten years after his father's death, Alex is resilient, with gratitude and appreciation for life.

Postvention in the American Death System

Postvention is best described as that part of the American death system which helps promote healing and reduce risk after a death by suicide through the use of people, places, times, objects, and symbols connected to death (Kastenbaum, 2012). A suicide loss survivor lives in a community and is part of a society in which certain components relate to death, dying, and bereavement. There is no one-size-fits-all solution to coping after a suicide occurs within a community. However, people, places, times, objects, and symbols in the death system can help the community understand the problem of suicide and offer assistance that fits the community's specific needs.

People in the death system are a coroner, a funeral director, an insurance agent, and a florist. A member of the clergy who offers religious support to a bereaved family, or a clinician who was working with a client who died by suicide are also people in the death system. There are also LOSS Teams that consist of people who are trained survivors (Campbell, n.d.). These people go to the scene of suicides to distribute information about resources. Other people in the death system are employed by organizations dedicated to suicide awareness such as the American Association of Suicidology (AAS), the American Foundation for Suicide Prevention (AFSP), Suicide Prevention Action Network (SPAN), and Suicide Awareness Voices of Education (SAVE).

Places in the death system are hospital emergency departments where a suicidal person is brought and a life might be saved. Hospitals are places where families are hopeful that their loved one will survive a suicide attempt. In these same places, they may be given the bad news that their loved one has died. Other places in the death system include funeral homes, cemeteries, and memorials— places where the bereaved come together as a group to commemorate the deceased.

Postvention is facilitated when suicide loss survivors attend formal and informal programs, go online for information and support, and connect with others in bereavement support groups. According to Shields, Russo, & Kavanagh (2019), suicide survivor loss support groups:

- may play a positive role in bereavement,

- give survivors a space to discuss their loss narrative,

- allow survivors to openly express emotions with others similarly bereaved,

- are most helpful when members are at various points in bereavement, so those newly bereaved find hope from those further along in their grief,

- work best after the shock has been worked through, so as not to become overcome by strong feelings of other group members, and

- need facilitators who are adequately trained in suicide survivor loss bereavement.

In addition, there are virtual places in the death system that support those bereaved by suicide. Carla Sofka coined the term, *thanatechnology*, which refers to communication technology used to provide death education, grief counseling, and thanatology research through the Internet (Sofka, Gilbert, & Noppe Cupit, 2012). Digital technology makes support available to suicide loss survivors through social media and social networking sites, online memorials, and virtual grief counseling. Online memorials honor the person who died, whereas virtual grief counseling offers support via computer or phone to those bereaved by suicide.

Times in the death system include dates such as the anniversary of a death, which help individuals remember loved ones they have lost to suicide. World Suicide Prevention Day (September 10) annually recognizes suicide survivors worldwide. On International Suicide Survivors of Loss Day (November 23), suicide loss survivors from around the world offer hope and encouragement to one another in events that take place in their own community.

Objects in the death system include an obituary placed in a local newspaper, or a death certificate that is given to a family member. Objects in the death system also include the means of suicide. A firearm is the most common means of suicide; a rope used to cause suffocation is the second-most-common means of suicide, and pills used to overdose are the third leading cause of suicide (CDC, 2018). Objects in the death system also include publications used to educate and inform such as the National Strategy for Suicide Prevention (US Department of Health and Human Services [HHS], 2001).

Symbols in the death system are varied. Some symbols are sensory, such as the solemn music and dark clothing associated with funerals or memorials. Other symbols are linguistic. Euphemisms such as *resting in peace* or *called home* are often used instead of the more emotionally-charged term *death*. Phrases such as *completed suicide* or *successful suicide* inappropriately imply criminality or sin. The non-stigmatizing terms *died by suicide* or *died of suicide* are more consistent with how individuals describe other types of deaths (e.g., *died of cancer* or *died by accident*) and are preferable to the term *committed suicide*.

When a Client Dies by Suicide

Suicide loss survivors have a difficult time coping with their loss. Among the bereaved are clinicians who struggle in suicide's aftermath. Marian Joyce, a psychologist, describes her experience working with a client for a year and a half. After her client died by suicide, she felt distress and questioned her competence as a therapist when her supervisor said, "Well, why don't we go over your case session by session so we can find out what went wrong?" (Joyce, n.d.). Therefore, postvention efforts need to focus on clinicians who have experienced a client's death by suicide and address its effects on their physical and mental health. Therapists may feel as though they are to blame when they review the patient's case with their supervisor.

Also, in the story, Sherry recognizes that Bill's therapist is shattered by the suicide when he calls her to offer his condolences. After making the decision to call Bill's family, the therapist needed to think through what he was going to say, and how much information about Bill he was going to provide to Sherry. The therapist could not know whether Sherry would wail into the phone, blame him for the suicide, or threaten litigation. It took courage for the clinician to call Sherry to support her, explain his thoughts about suicide, and the contact he had with Bill prior to his death.

According to Stene-Larsen & Reneflot, "contact with primary health care was highest in the year prior to suicide with an average contact rate of 80%. At one month, the average rate was 44%. The lifetime contact rate for mental health care was 57%, and 31% in the final 12 months" (2017, p. 1).

According to the American Psychiatric Association (n.d.), therapists who decide to call a family member may be concerned that what they say, or the manner in which it is said, will affect the likelihood of being sued. Therapists who have experienced the suicide of a client may also be concerned about clinical competence, organizational protocols, reaction of colleagues, stigmatization, ethical guidelines, as well as their own grief process, posttraumatic stress, self-compassion, resilience, personal growth and posttraumatic growth. The following questions would be appropriate for the therapist's consideration.

Bill's therapist called Sherry to offer his condolences. While speaking with Bill's widow, the therapist might have had one or more of the following questions whirling through his mind:

- How has the suicide of his client affected his clinical competence?

- Has the death clouded his clinical decision-making?

- Does his organization have protocols in place that offer him emotional support?

- Will his organization's investigation of his client's sessions affect his sense of professional security?

- Are his colleagues being personally supportive or are they staying away?

- Does he feel professionally isolated in the workplace?

- Is he hiding what happened from his colleagues?

- Have the therapist's colleagues ever shared their personal experience of a suicide of a client?

- What ethical guidelines did the therapist set up for himself prior to calling the client's family member?

- Why was it important for him to call his client's bereaved family member as soon as possible?

- Was he careful not to say anything over the phone that would make him appear guilty?

- Is he being empathetic and compassionate as he listens to the bereaved family member?

- What could possibly happen if the bereaved family member feels that the therapist is being unfeeling, detached, or callous?

- If he fears litigation, what is causing his apprehension?

- What emotional, physical, cognitive, behavioral, or spiritual grief reactions could he possibly be experiencing?

- Why could he possibly experience disenfranchised grief?

- Is the stigma related to a client's death by suicide increasing his stress level?

- In what way can he rethink what happened to manage any negative thoughts?

- What is the source of the therapist's attitude regarding the suicide of his client?

- How can the therapist maintain job satisfaction at such a frustrating time in his professional career?

- In what ways can he be self-compassionate during this critical time?

- What professional transformation (e.g., support other clinician survivors) can take place when a client dies by suicide?

- How can he build his personal resilience after a client dies by suicide?

- Can he now have a closer relationship with his colleagues or a new opportunity in suicide awareness because he has experienced personal growth or posttraumatic growth?

Consider what happens emotionally and physically when clinicians ask themselves these questions. According to Ting, Sanders, Jacobson & Power (2006), clinicians whose clients died by suicide reported feelings of grief and secondary traumatic stress, such as denial, anger, avoidance, intrusion, responsibility, and isolation. Immediate traumatic symptoms can include shock, numbing, and dissociation, and later traumatic responses can include intrusive thoughts and images of their client's death (Plakun & Tillman, 2005). Farberow (2005) notes that clinicians may experience a loss of self-esteem and doubt their skills.

Finlayson & Simmonds (2019) found that clinicians who lose a client to suicide need to be able to openly communicate their loss at work with peer assistance; have room to grieve; and a chance to get involved and learn more about suicide. In a study by Sherba, Linley, Coxe & Gersper (2019), clinicians reported that their agency or practice should have made a stronger effort to assist them after the suicide of their client. Generally, beneficial coping responses in clinicians include talking to a supervisor and colleagues, and recognizing that they are not responsible for the death (Finlayson & Simmonds, 2018).

PART 2

The Story

CHAPTER 1

THE WORST DAY

When my alarm clock woke me, I had no idea that, at the age of eleven, I was about to have the worst day of my life. It started out pretty much normal. My five-year-old sister, Debbie, was wearing her favorite pink dress and eating cereal as she watched TV. Dad was sitting at the kitchen table. That's when I noticed something odd. Dad wasn't drinking his coffee or reading the paper. He was staring at the TV screen; he hardly ever watched cartoons with Debbie. When I asked him what was going on, he said he was taking the day off. I thought it was weird but didn't say anything. I was late. I grabbed my backpack and lunch and hurried out the door and down the street to wait for the school bus.

It was eleven o'clock in the morning when the principal came into the classroom and whispered something to my teacher. My teacher told me to get my books and backpack and go downstairs to the office with the principal. I couldn't imagine what I had done wrong, but I silently followed behind the principal. When I got to the office, I noticed that Uncle Sammy was sitting by the window. He was looking at his hands. When he saw me, he quickly got up and told me we had to get home. I started to get worried.

"Uncle Sammy, why are you picking me up from school? What's going on?"

"We have to go. Now, Alex," he said and headed for the door.

Uncle Sammy sounded angry. I had never seen him like that before. "I don't get it. You're taking me home? Is something wrong? Where are Mom and Dad?"

My uncle didn't answer my questions.

We rushed to my uncle's truck. Strong, cold gusts of wind almost knocked us down. When we finally reached the truck and slid inside, Uncle Sammy just sat there for a moment, jingling his keys and not looking at me. He was usually upbeat and fun. Something wasn't right.

"Your mom asked me to come get you," he said. "Something happened. Something big, something really . . . really . . . I'll explain it all to you at home." My uncle was shivering as he started the truck. My teeth were chattering. He turned up the heat, but it didn't make me feel any warmer.

"Uncle Sammy? You look funny. What's going on?"

"Just stop, Alex! Let me concentrate on getting us home. Put your seat belt on, please."

"I want to know what happened; you have to tell me what happened!" Frustrated, I reached for my seat belt as Uncle Sammy backed out of the parking lot. We didn't even make it off the school grounds. Without saying a word, he drove to the side of the road, shut off the engine, and burst into tears.

"Oh my goodness, he's dead! He's . . ." Sobbing, he punched the steering wheel and whispered, "Your dad died this morning." He took a deep breath. "He killed himself."

My heart flipped over in my chest. I just stared at him, stunned. How could my dad be dead? I wanted to ask Uncle Sammy more questions, but I couldn't. Because suddenly I couldn't breathe, and I couldn't stop crying. Uncle Sammy wanted to calm me down. I know he did. But all we could do was cry together.

Finally, Uncle Sammy hugged me, kissed my forehead, and started the truck. The ride home took less than five minutes, but I don't remember any of it. I stared out the window. I felt as though I wasn't even in the truck, as if I were outside myself. This could not be happening to me.

Uncle Sammy parked in the driveway. I got out of the truck and slammed the door. It felt as though I was moving in slow motion, but my mind was racing. Was my dad really dead? Was this some awful dream? Would I wake up any minute? Although my uncle had told me that my dad had killed himself, part of me was still uncertain. With each step I took toward the house, my heart beat faster.

By the time I reached the front door, I was certain my heart would explode from my chest. Mom was on the phone, sitting at the kitchen table. Debbie was drawing a picture, and the table was covered in crayons. Later, I would learn that my mom's friend, Chris, picked Debbie up from kindergarten. Mom's face was puffy and her eyes were red. She was talking to someone about Dad. I heard her whisper, "Yes, military funeral honors; closed casket. Thank you."

When Mom saw me staring at her, she quickly hung up the phone. It was the most terrifying moment of my life. "Mom, what happened to Dad?" She got up from the table and hugged me tighter than she ever had before.

"Let's sit down on the sofa. I have to talk to you." We both sat down, and she whispered, "I have some very bad news. Dad killed himself."

"That's what Uncle Sammy said. I don't get it. Why would he do something like that?"

"I keep asking myself the same question," Mom replied as she softly rubbed my hand and looked around the room. "No matter what kind of problems he had, he never should have killed himself."

"Problems?"

"Problems that he couldn't manage, I guess. I don't know what he was thinking. He kept a lot inside. Maybe whatever he was thinking overwhelmed him this morning."

As much as I didn't want to ask her, I had to know. "How did he do it?"

I heard only some of the words Mom said. I was so confused. After she explained how he died, I screamed, "No, Mom, no! You're lying! That's a horrible lie."

"I'm not lying, Alex. I can't believe it either. Dad stayed home from work today, and he killed himself." Taking several deep breaths, Mom continued, "He'd taken his own life, Alex, and I couldn't save him."

"I don't believe it, Mom."

"I can't believe it, either. I called 911 right away. I tried to . . . I tried . . . I did CPR, but Dad was dead. The ambulance was here within minutes. There was nothing the emergency medical team could do to save him."

Why did my mom keep saying this? I wanted to see my dad.

"Where is he now? Where's Dad?"

"I believe that Dad is in heaven. His body has to be examined by a special medical doctor and will be taken to the funeral home later." As we sat on the sofa, Mom whispered, "Everything is going to be okay."

I said nothing. Mom held me tightly, but I felt stiff and unbending. Even though I very much wanted to hold on tight to her, I was angry. I pushed Mom away. Everything was not okay. Dad killed himself in the basement. I was mad at my mom for not going into the basement sooner. I was mad at whoever was making Dad have problems. I was mad at Dad for killing himself. I was mad at myself for being at school when he did it, when he needed me.

"I love you so much," Mom said as she began to cry. When my mom started to cry, I started to cry, and I couldn't stop. It felt as though we sat on that sofa for a long time. My mom held me and tried to explain what had happened. She wanted to make sure I was okay.

I wondered if any of this was my fault. "Mom, did Dad kill himself because of something I did?"

"Oh, Alex, no. Nothing you said or did could have ever caused your dad to do such a thing," Mom said. "Don't you ever forget that. Dad didn't leave a note. So, we will have to figure it all out ourselves. Alex, this did not happen because of anything you did or did not do!"

Although Mom gave me the basic facts about what had happened, she mostly focused on my feelings because she knew I blamed myself. No matter how much Mom reassured me that it wasn't my fault, I didn't truly believe her. I still needed answers. Was he angry at me for always asking him to help me with my homework? I knew something was different that morning. I should have stayed home. I told myself that everything was going to be okay, but I didn't believe a word of it.

Ten Years Later

There it was. In my cellphone calendar. Today was the anniversary of my dad's death. What was so bad that he would have killed himself? Although I'm turning twenty-one, I still feel like that eleven-year-old boy, and I'm still asking myself the same questions. Only my dad knows why he took his life. His death was not the result of one single event. I still wish that he had sought help: called a crisis hotline, reached out to his family, or figured out some way to cope with whatever he was going through.

My family didn't try to hide the fact that my dad took his own life. We still talk about what he did and the impact it has had on our lives. One lesson that I have learned from all of this is: adults need to be honest with kids about what happened. It seemed that everyone was telling me something different. I remember that Uncle Sammy was angry. Mom was trying to take control of the situation, and my sister was totally confused. I can still see the sad face of the school secretary as I walked into the school office.

As a kid, I thought I might have caused my father to kill himself. That was a problem for me. I believed that, somehow, I was to blame. I had to sort out all the facts about what happened. I focused on the meaning of each detail. I needed to put it all in perspective. It took time but I was eventually able to change my belief about blame because it simply did not fit the facts. The facts were: I was just a kid, my mom had no idea my dad would kill himself, we didn't know the signs to look for, and we never imagined that my father would take his own life.

Follow-Up Questions

- In what ways can you relate to the family in Chapter 1?

- Have you had an experience similar to Alex's, or if not similar to Alex's, has someone very close to you died?

- What was your relationship with the person who died?

- How old were you when this person died?

- Where were you when this person died?

- Who told you that this person had died?

- What did that person (or other people) tell you about how the death had occurred?

- What did you feel toward the person who told you about the death?

- What did the loss of your loved one mean to you?

- What lesson did the loss teach you about life?

- Alex's personality traits (e.g., honest, curious) helped him cope in the immediate aftermath. What did you learn about your strengths as you coped with your loss?

CHAPTER 2

The Next Day

Before my dad's death, I had a certain routine every morning. I would start my day thinking about the kind of cereal I would eat for breakfast. This day was different. When I woke up, my first thoughts were all about Dad. He was dead. He would not be lighting the fireplace. Dad always lit the fireplace. Did my mom even know how to light it?

As I walked into the kitchen, I found Uncle Sammy sitting in my dad's chair eating cereal. I thought about how my dad would never again be sitting in his chair reading the newspaper and drinking coffee from his favorite mug. That was his routine. Dad and I loved eating cereal. We would fill up a bowl and read the cereal box. It was our routine. It felt weird knowing that my dad would never again eat his cereal sitting beside me. I sat down, feeling anxious.

My sister, Debbie, handed me one of the *Princess in Black* books. "Read to me, Alex." The book, a birthday present, had a picture of a girl wearing a black superhero costume and cape.

"Hey, Deb, didn't you wear a costume like this for Halloween?" I asked. "It almost looks like the Batgirl costume you wore."

"Yeah," Debbie said with a giggle, making me smile.

"I'll read it to you later today. I promise. First, let me eat my cereal."

"You promise?" Deb asked.

"I promise." I poured my cereal and dug in. As I ate, I told my uncle and my mom about last night. It had been a strange night. I had had a bad headache and felt mixed up inside. I wondered: Was I always going to feel this way? I wanted to go to sleep and wake up and find out it never happened, that Dad wasn't dead.

During the night, something woke me. I thought I saw Dad standing by my bed. I knew he couldn't actually be in my room, but it felt like he was there. As soon as I got up, he was gone. I went back to sleep. The last thing I thought about as I fell asleep was seeing Dad at the kitchen table the morning he died. He wasn't reading the paper. He wasn't drinking coffee. Maybe I should have known then that something was wrong.

Sitting at the breakfast table, I felt scared. I didn't know what I was afraid of. I was confused and angry and sad all at once. It felt like a typical morning in my house, but at the same time, nothing felt the same. While eating breakfast, Uncle Sammy looked through our photo album. He had tears in his eyes, but a smile on his face.

I thought about the times Dad and I would insert new photos in the album. We had a routine for this, too. He sat in his favorite chair, and I handed him the photos. One by one, Dad placed each photo in the album. Then, while Mom and Debbie looked over our work, Dad would say, "Let's go play ball, Champ," and we would play catch in the backyard. When I was little, Dad gave me the nickname "Champ." I will never forget how special that name had made me feel.

"Uncle Sammy, I keep thinking Dad will come home soon. I can't stop thinking about him."

"I'm thinking about him, too."

"Me, too," Mom said.

After breakfast, I sat down on the sofa with Debbie to watch TV. Mom and Uncle Sammy were washing dishes. I wasn't trying to listen to their conversation, but from what I could hear, they were talking about real estate and bills.

Uncle Sammy looked over at me and said, "Somebody's awfully quiet."

"Dad had promised me he was going to watch me in the school play next week," I said. "My class is putting on a play for the entire grade. All the parents are invited."

"What's it about?"

"The play is about the Constitution. I'll be talking about the judicial part of the government."

"Aw, man," Uncle Sammy exclaimed, "your dad always talked about how good you were in your school plays and how you never missed a line. I know your dad would have loved to see you in the play."

I felt angry. "If my dad had loved seeing me school plays, he wouldn't have killed himself. If he had loved me . . ." The more we talked about it, the angrier I felt.

Uncle Sammy sat next to me and said, "I get what you're saying. That wasn't supposed to happen. Your dad is supposed to be here and go to your school play."

"But it did happen, Uncle Sammy. I don't get it. One day Dad was here and the next day he's gone. Just the other day he helped me when I practiced my lines. We worked on my part together. He killed himself before my play. That doesn't make any sense."

"I know. This is hard for any of us to understand."

"I wish he hadn't died."

"Me too. I wish that he hadn't done what he did . . . I wish he had gotten help," Uncle Sammy said. "It's important to always reach out if you're considering hurting yourself." Uncle Sammy looked at his hands. They were big, like Dad's. "He must have felt so helpless. He should have reached out if he was hurting that much. He wasn't thinking clearly. It doesn't make sense."

My uncle explained, "Maybe he had tunnel vision. Maybe he just could not see a light at the end of a tunnel. He should have talked to me about whatever he was feeling . . . he didn't have to suffer in silence. He knew that I would have helped him get back to his old self."

"I know you would have, Uncle Sammy."

"I would have made sure that he had the will to live. But maybe he isolated himself from me because he didn't want me to do that for him."

Mom walked into the room and sat down next to Debbie. My mind was spinning with *if onlys*. *If only* I had stayed home from school yesterday, maybe I could have stopped him. *If only* I had been nicer to Dad, maybe he wouldn't have died of suicide. I was worrying about things I had never thought about before. I turned to my mom. "Mom, could I have done something to save Dad?"

"Oh Alex, you couldn't have predicted that he would end his life. None of us could have."

Suddenly, Uncle Sammy slapped his big hands on his legs. "Hey, I have an idea. How about we go out for some hot cocoa?"

Mom, taken off guard, asked, "Who? You and the kids?"

"No, all four of us can go out for hot cocoa. No matter how long we all sit around with our heads down, feeling like this, nothing is going to change. Maybe you and the kids need some Montana air. The sun has come out. Let's get out of the house."

"It's freezing outside!" Mom said.

Debbie begged, "Please, Mom. Let's take a ride and get hot cocoa." Mom agreed and went upstairs with Debbie to get dressed.

I blurted out, "Uncle Sammy, was it my fault?"

"Your fault?"

"Maybe I should have been a better kid."

"A better kid?"

"Yeah, maybe I shouldn't have asked Dad so many questions about the branches of government this week. I should have known. *If only* I had stayed home from school and done something."

"I can see that you are struggling with whether your dad's death was your fault. Listen, your dad obviously had bigger problems than any of us were aware of," Uncle Sammy assured me.

"Mom should have done something to prevent it."

"Do you think Mom had had an idea he was going to take his own life?"

"No, I don't think, so."

"Hadn't she been doing laundry?" Uncle Sammy asked.

"Yeah, but maybe Mom should have checked on him sooner."

"Your dad went into the basement so she would not see him. Was it your mom's fault because she had been doing laundry?" he asked.

"I'm still mad at her. I'm mad at Dad. He should be here. He should be going to my school play next week. Every dad will be there but him!"

"That's a tough break," Uncle Sammy said. "I'm really sorry your dad won't be there. I'm glad you're talking to me about your feelings, Alex. Can I go to your school and watch you in your play next week?"

"Yeah, sure." It would be fine for my uncle to watch me in the play, I thought, but I wanted my dad to be there. I felt angry that my uncle would be there and not my dad. "I'll let you know the day and time, Uncle Sammy. But I don't know if I'll still be in the same school."

"Same school? Why wouldn't you be in the same school?" Uncle Sammy looked puzzled.

"I don't know. We might have to move because Mom can't afford to pay the bills."

"Wow, bills! What on earth would put that idea in your head?" My uncle stared at the floor and thought for a few seconds. It was no secret in our family that at times I was known for listening to the grown-up conversations. Dad had said I was smart because I was always listening to the adults around me. He had said I was a real Einstein.

"There's no problem with finances, Alex," Uncle Sammy said. "Your mom can afford to live in your house with you and your sister. It's important for you to feel safe. I love you, your mother, and Deb so much. I promise you that I'm here to look out for all of you. Everything will be fine."

As I listened to Uncle Sammy, I thought to myself: everything is not fine. My dad's dead! On the other hand, I had to trust Uncle Sammy and Mom and all the adults who loved me that they would keep me safe.

Before I knew it, Mom and Debbie were coming down the stairs. I pulled on my coat and boots and we headed out for hot cocoa.

We went to the same diner that Dad used to take us to. It felt strange sitting in the booth without him. On the way home, we stopped at a store and bought more hot cocoa. At home, Mom, Uncle Sammy, and Debbie went inside, but I stayed outside to fly my helicopter. It had a cockpit cabin and a strobe light. My dad had taught me how to use the transmitter and how to fix the blades. After a while, my hands were cold; they felt as though they were frozen to the radio control. So, I went inside for some more hot cocoa.

As I walked into the kitchen, Mom yelled at me, "Please get your helicopter off the table. We don't have any room in here for food, let alone helicopters." Mom was right. The kitchen was filled with flowers and large baskets of fruit. Three tuna casseroles sat in the refrigerator. The kitchen smelled awful—a combination of tuna fish and flowers. About an hour later, Dad's doctor called to speak with Mom. After they spoke, she stared out the kitchen window and said, "The doctor did the right thing in calling me to offer his condolences."

"What's that mean, Mom? Condolences?"

"Condolence is an expression of sympathy. It's part of our culture. Friends and neighbors show that they care about us by sending food, flowers, and cards. They call us on the phone, email us, or they visit."

Just then, the doorbell rang. It was Uncle Alan and Aunt Jillian. Uncle Alan was Dad's youngest brother. They stood in the hall, taking turns hugging Mom and Uncle Sammy. My aunt and uncle lived in Las Vegas. Mom and Dad had fun whenever they visited them. My dad had promised me that he would take me to Las Vegas when I turned twenty-one. He would not be keeping that promise.

As I hugged my aunt and uncle, I was shocked at how similar Uncle Alan was to Dad. Debbie ran into the hall and gave everyone hugs. Debbie wanted to show Aunt Jillian and Uncle Alan photos from Disney World. Only a few months had passed since we'd all been together on that fun Florida vacation. But now, it seems like such a long time ago.

"Oh yeah, show us the photos," Uncle Alan said as he and my aunt sat down on the sofa in the den.

As Debbie went to get the album, Uncle Alan grabbed a handful of nuts and a pear from one of the fruit baskets. He spoke softly to my mom, "How are you, Sherry? How are the kids holding up?"

"What can I say? This is definitely the worst of times." Mom shook her head. "He's dead, Alan. My husband, my friend, my world—he's gone forever. How could he do this to me? I don't understand. Why would he kill himself?"

I sat on the sofa pretending to watch TV, but I was really listening to the adults.

"Bill must have felt helpless. Did you speak with his therapist?" Aunt Jillian asked.

"Uh-huh. We spoke on the phone. He felt terrible about what happened. I asked him how … why …. He told me that more than a quarter of the patients who kill themselves have seen their mental health professional during the previous two months for a mental health issue. He said something like 30%. It's common to have contact with primary health care prior to dying by suicide even in the final month before a person takes their own life."

"Bill's therapist should have prevented the suicide," Aunt Jillian said.

"I'm sure he did what he could. He was really sorry it happened. I felt comforted by what he said."

"Well, I'm angry with the doctor. He should have seen this coming," Aunt Jillian said.

"We were all blindsided by this. The doctor is struggling with the fact that his patient died by suicide. He sounded genuinely sad," Mom said.

Uncle Alan said, "Probably because he cared about Bill. Maybe he's grieving."

"We're all grieving," Mom said.

"Truthfully, we can sit here and try to figure it all out, but in the end, we all did the best we could with what we had," Aunt Jillian sighed.

"And what was that?" Mom asked in between sniffles.

My aunt got up and wrapped her arm around Mom's shoulders. "Our love. We gave Bill our love," my aunt whispered.

Uncle Alan said, "Yeah, we sure did."

"Only Bill knows the reason he ended his life. We have to live with that," Aunt Jillian added.

Uncle Alan and Mom started to cry as Aunt Jillian comforted them both. Debbie came back into the room with her album. We looked at the photos. Mom started to laugh as she saw the photo of Dad wearing Mickey Mouse ears.

Touching my arm, Uncle Alan said, "Your dad seemed happy. You never would have known the extreme stress he must have been going through, his state of mind. He didn't have the skills to cope with what he was dealing with. I don't know what he was thinking, Alex. I'm so sorry."

Ten Years Later

I have let go of much of the anger I felt right after my dad died and I no longer feel guilty about having been unable to prevent his death. I realize that I had done nothing wrong. I had had no idea my dad was going to take his life. Also, I had felt shame after my father died. I didn't have a dad like the other kids. I didn't want to be the kid without a dad. I had been embarrassed because other fathers were alive and mine was dead. I no longer feel that shame.

I told only one person at college about my dad's suicide. I guess I still felt embarrassed. My good friend, Lori, a college senior, had attempted suicide three years before we met. Lori told me that now she had a safety plan, one she had worked on with her therapist. She had written down ways to cope in the event that she had thoughts of killing herself. She had also written down a list of skills she could use to help her deal with whatever she might be going through.

Lori asked me if she could write down my name as someone to reach out to if she ever thought about killing herself. Lori knows that I would do anything I could to make sure that she did not take her life. If she needed me, I would support her and get her through whatever crisis she was in. You don't have to be a professional to help another person. A simple act of kindness can save the life of someone in crisis.

Lori told me that when she attempted suicide, she had every intention of dying, just like my dad. Lori called what happened to her a "lived experience." She has a better understanding of suicide, having lived through her own suicide attempt. Now Lori and a therapist are working together to educate people in the community about preventing suicide. In their presentations, they discuss medications Lori was taking at the time of her attempt, what she thought of her therapist at the time, and what the hospitalization was like for her.

Lori wants to get her masters and doctorate degrees in psychology. She has lots of reasons to live and can teach all of us a few things about being hopeful, something I guess my dad didn't feel when he ended his life. Lori says it is important that professionals get suicide awareness training, which covers how to assess a suicide, provide treatment, and identify risk factors. After Lori's suicide attempt, the hospital did a great job following up with her through emails. She calls this a *caring contact*. Although she never responded, Lori says she knew that the hospital staff was really concerned about her and that made her feel good.

A few weeks ago, Lori took me to a diner. People at our table just wanted to talk about death. She called it a death café. I didn't tell any of them about my dad. I did listen a lot and shared some of my own ideas about death. Driving back to campus, I told Lori about the phone call my mom had received from the therapist immediately after my dad died. Lori wondered whether Dad's doctor had received training in managing suicide risk in his patients, or just training in treating mental illness. According to Lori, evidence shows that training specific to suicide makes a difference. She says there is no reason for any mental health professional to apply outdated training that could be potentially harmful to patients. Lori is going to be an awesome therapist.

Follow-Up Questions

- In what ways can you relate to the family in Chapter 2?

- If you had a certain routine that changed after your loved one died, how did it change, either for the better or for the worse?

- If you felt your loved one's presence after their death, what was that like for you? Do you think this is unusual or strange?

- Do you have any special pictures of your loved one?

- Right now, what are you most worried about?

- Are your family members worried about any of the same things that you are worried about? If so, what are your family members worried about and how are they coping?

- What was the hardest time for you after your loved one's death?

- Has the death of your loved one changed your world view?

- Alex's personality traits (e.g., trusting, intelligent) helped him cope in the days following his dad's death. What did you learn about your strengths as you coped with your loss?

CHAPTER 3

Mourning

My Aunt Jillian and Uncle Alan sat on the sofa, dressed in black, while Debbie played a game on my aunt's phone. Mom and Uncle Sammy were in the kitchen, also dressed in black.

"Mom, why is everyone wearing black?" I asked.

Mom responded, "I should have talked to you about this before. I take so many things for granted. How would you know about our mourning custom when I haven't told you about it?"

"Mourning?"

"Yes, mourning. Mo-U-r-ning. It's not the same word as when you get up in the morning. Mourning is how we express our grief. It's how we behave or respond to being sad because Dad died. Mourning rituals show people that someone close to us has died. Although we have our own family culture, we are influenced by values and beliefs of religion and spirituality. Every culture has certain traditions when it comes to expressing grief."

"Like what, Mom?"

"Like wearing black, for one thing. It's a mourning ritual. I think it goes way back to Victorian times. Another mourning ritual is the act of giving food to a friend or family in grief."

"That's why we received all those fruit baskets and tuna casseroles," Uncle Sammy said.

"Exactly. Neighbors and friends care about us," Mom said. "Bringing food to our home is a mourning custom. People who care about us may send flowers or donate money to a charity in memory of Dad. For instance, Dad's office sent a donation in his memory to an organization that helps prevent suicide."

"That's nice, Mom."

"One of Dad's coworkers stopped by on his way home from work. He gave me a picture of Dad that had been taken at his company's Christmas party. Dad was dressed up as an elf!"

"You've got to be kidding. Mom! I have to see it."

Uncle Sammy laughed at the memory. "Bill bought that elf outfit with me about a week before Christmas. It had green shorts, a big red collar, two buttons that looked like peppermint candy, and red- and white-striped tights. He wore the floppy red and green hat in the truck on the way home from the store."

Mom said, "I'll show you the picture, Alex. I thought we might take it out each December to remember the funny things your dad used to do. I'd like for it to become a ritual for us. It's a nice way to remember Dad."

"I like that idea," I said. "What other rituals can we do, Mom?"

"We can light a candle with Debbie and say a prayer or recite a poem. This could be our family ritual."

"I'd like that, too."

"Of course you only light candles when adults are with you."

"I know. Can we do it today?"

"Sure. We can do it whenever we need to. We can take out the photo album and view it together."

"Will these rituals make us feel better, Mom?"

"The intention behind these rituals is not only to remember, but to celebrate Dad's life. It's a way to continue to feel connected to him," Mom said.

Uncle Sammy said, "Alex, you and your dad had a really strong bond."

Mom nodded, "That bond is not broken because he's dead. It's good to keep memories alive, Alex, like you do in your scrapbook of report cards and awards. Maybe you could add some of Dad's things to your scrapbook. Would you like that?"

"Yeah, I would."

"I'll give you Dad's driver's license and some pictures of him."

"I would like that. Thanks."

"I might have a couple of things for you, too," Uncle Sammy said.

I went to my room and grabbed my scrapbook from the shelf. I started writing words that reminded me of Dad at the top of some of the pages, I wrote, *"Sports Dad Liked," "Dad's Hobbies," "Dad's Favorite Animals,"* and *"Dad's Favorite Food."*

Later, I sat on the sofa with my mom and showed her the scrapbook as she drank a cup of tea. She read what I wrote about Dad's favorite animals. He loved the zoo, I thought. I'm going to need tons of pages to show all of the animals he liked.

"Mom, can we go to the zoo in the spring and take some photos of Dad's favorite animals, especially the monkeys?"

"We'll plan for it. I know that you like the snakes, geckos, and scorpions."

"And the lizards, too. I wish Dad could go. Remember when the monkey kept pointing at the banana Dad was eating? Too funny."

Mom said, "That was hysterical. Dad will certainly be there with us, in spirit."

I looked over at my uncle and realized that he was sitting in my dad's chair. My mom calls it a winged chair, but my dad always called it his "king" chair. "Uncle Sammy, I wonder if I'll always see that chair as Dad's chair."

"When I sat down," said Uncle Sammy, "I immediately thought of the many conversations I had with your dad while he was sitting in his 'king' chair." He thought for a moment. "Sitting here makes me feel close to Bill. I miss my brother so much."

Mom then asked my uncle if he wanted to deliver the eulogy at Dad's funeral. While he was thinking about what she said, Mom explained to me that a eulogy is where Uncle Sammy would talk about his brother in front of everyone. Uncle Sammy was worried that he would break down and not be able to get the words out.

"Sammy, Bill would have wanted you to speak at his service," Mom said.

"I don't know what to say, Sherry."

"Focus on what you admired most about him. Share a funny story. Share the elf story. Tell everyone what it was that made you two so close," Mom said.

Uncle Sammy raised his voice, "So close? Admire? But I'm so angry at what Bill did. He should have come to me. Admiring my brother is the last thing on my mind."

"I know you're angry. We're all shattered by this. Believe me. I mean . . . I lost the light of my life. He was your brother. For crying out loud, he was my husband!" I watched her as she took a deep breath and cooled down. Pouring another cup of tea, Mom softened her tone. "Please, Sammy, in the long run, you will be glad you did the eulogy."

"I'll never be glad again. Oh man, I miss him," Uncle Sammy sighed, sinking deeper into the chair.

"Uncle Sammy, I'll help you," I said. "I have lots of memories of you and Dad teaching me about baseball, and going fishing, or to the movies."

"That would be tons of memories," Uncle Sammy smiled. "I'll work on it. I'll come up with something. Maybe I'll talk about what I'll miss the most about him. I can do it."

"Sam, you'll be fine; the eulogy should be only about ten minutes long," Mom said.

"Uncle Sammy, write down what you want to say first. That's what I do before I work on a speech that I have to give to my class."

"Good idea, Alex," Uncle Sammy said.

We all sat at the kitchen table, silently, thinking about Dad and the funeral. Finally, Uncle Sammy asked, "Alex, are you nervous about the funeral? Do you have any questions?"

"I've pictured what's going to happen at the funeral. Mom explained it all to me already, but I'm still nervous."

With a grin for Mom, Uncle Sammy asked, "What did your mom tell you?"

"We'll be going to the funeral home. That's where Dad's body is. His body will be in a box, a casket."

"I don't know if I'm ready for that," Uncle Sammy admitted.

"Me neither, Uncle Sammy. The casket will be kept closed at the service and then placed in a special car called a hearse. Then the hearse will be driven to the cemetery."

"Right. All the cars going to the cemetery will follow behind the hearse, and all of them will keep their headlights on," Uncle Sammy explained. "You, your mom, and Debbie will be in the first car behind the hearse."

"It's called a funeral procession. It's a time to honor your dad," Mom added, then leaned over and hugged me. She whispered, "I gave you a lot of information about Dad's funeral. I hope it makes it easier for you to understand what will take place."

"It's smart preparing him for the funeral, Sherry. This way he knows what to expect at the service and at the grave," Uncle Sammy said.

Deb, Aunt Jillian, and Uncle Alan came into the kitchen. Deb still had Aunt Jillian's phone. "She's trying to solve a puzzle," Aunt Jillian said.

"This is a fun game," Debbie said, then looked up. "What's a grave?"

My sister had been listening to us while she played. I responded, "It's a large hole dug in the ground. Dad's casket will be put into a grave."

"Yeah, that's it. The cemetery workers will cover the casket with dirt after we leave," Uncle Sammy said.

"How can Daddy breathe if he's covered in dirt? Won't that hurt him?" Debbie asked.

"Deb, Daddy's body doesn't work anymore. He doesn't breathe. He doesn't feel anything," Mom explained.

As she finished her tea, Mom mentioned that some people at the funeral will be crying. Some people will be praying. Some people will not say anything at all.

"Then we'll return home and it'll be over," Uncle Sammy sighed.

Mom continued to explain things, "After the funeral, everyone will gather at our home, eat, and share their loss—Dad's death. When we go back to the cemetery in a few months, there will be a headstone over the grave. We talked about this already. I want to make sure you know what to expect."

"I know, Mom. I've seen headstones in movies."

"Dad's name, birthday, and date of death will be engraved on the headstone," Mom said. "I'm considering the words, *Loving Husband, Father, Son, and Brother.*"

"I appreciate your putting the word *brother* on the stone," Uncle Sammy said.

Uncle Alan added, "Me, too."

"He loved you both," Mom whispered.

Uncle Sammy bit his lip and tried not to cry; Uncle Alan just shook his head.

Mom turned to me and said, "Alex, you can put something into the casket."

I had not thought of this. I asked, "Can I put two rocks in the casket, one metamorphic and one igneous?"

"Meta . . . what?" Mom asked, confused.

"Rocks, Mom. I'm talking about rocks. Dad would understand," I whispered.

"Yeah, I know he would," Uncle Sammy said.

"I have a picture of me and Dad fishing. I want him to have it."

"I'll make sure the rocks and the picture are placed in his casket. Debbie is going to draw a picture and have that placed in the casket too," Mom said.

"Is Debbie going to the funeral?" Aunt Jillian asked.

"Yes," Mom said. "I believe that no child is too young to attend a funeral, especially if the person who died is their dad. I've explained everything to Debbie, so she won't be afraid or confused. But I have to keep repeating the same explanations to her, over and over again."

Uncle Alan said, "This is hard for a five-year-old to understand. It's hard for all of us, no matter how old we are. Grieving is painful."

"People have told me that I'm like President Kennedy's wife in the way I grieve," Aunt Jillian said.

"What do you mean?" Mom asked.

"I don't cry at funerals. I feel grief intensely and keep thinking about the person who died. I put all of my energy into doing something."

"Like what?" I asked.

"I need to take action," Aunt Jillian said. "I'm the type of person who makes the funeral arrangements or sets up a memorial fund. I just need to do something tangible. You remember when my mom died last year of breast cancer? I sat with my dad and my sisters on the sofa. They were crying and went through tons of tissues. I don't think I even grabbed a single one. I sat there untangling my mom's jewelry. Although I couldn't fix my mom, I could fix her tangled necklaces."

"Yeah, I remember telling you then that you didn't need to untangle her necklaces," Mom said.

"But I *did* need to do exactly that at the time," Aunt Jillian responded.

I watched as my mom rocked Debbie in her arms like a baby. I had not seen her do that in a very long time. After a while, Debbie wanted to go outside and play in the snow before it got dark. I volunteered to take her. We got on our jackets, hats, and gloves and ran for the door. When we came back in, Mom had hot cocoa waiting. I gave her the rocks and picture for my dad.

Ten Years Later

I love going to the movies. My dad and I used to go to them all the time. At college, my friends and I go to the movies a lot. Sometimes there's a scene in which one of the characters dies by suicide. My friends probably don't think twice about it, but that scene kind of ruins the movie for me. I get very upset. But I don't say anything to my friends because they have no clue that my father died that way. I wonder if I'm the only person who has lost a loved one to suicide who feels this way.

Two weeks ago, Lori and I went to a movie in which the actor was trying to figure out a solution to something. He kept asking questions and repeatedly claiming how it was unsolvable. I kept thinking about why my dad killed himself and how *that* question is unsolvable. Did he have a criminal or legal problem that he hadn't shared with anyone? Had he had an argument with my mom or someone else? Perhaps I would be better off asking myself what motivates me to keep asking "why, why, why" and what any possible answer would mean to me.

Lori says that I have engaged in magical thinking after my dad died because I believed that there was a link between my going to school the day he died and my dad taking his life. My logic and my perception were off. Even so, every now and then, I wonder if I could have done something to prevent my dad's suicide.

- In what ways can you relate to the family in Chapter 3?

- What mourning customs does your family observe?

- If you created a ritual after your loved one died, what was it?

- If you could deliver a eulogy for this person now, what would you say?

- In what ways have you honored your loved one who died?

- What is your favorite memory of your loved one?

- Should young children be allowed to attend a funeral?

- Were you told everything you needed to know about funerals before attending your first one?

- If you attended the funeral, what was the hardest part for you?

- If you or anyone else placed something special in the casket, describe it.

- What motivates you to continue the bond with your loved one?

- Have you been able to make sense out of your loved one's death and pieced together features of their life and death to comprehend the loss?

- What have you learned about the way you grieve compared to how others around you grieve?

- Alex's personality traits (e.g., kind, confident, optimistic) helped him cope with the funeral planning. What strengths helped, or are helping you cope with the death of your loved one?

CHAPTER 4

TELLING A FRIEND WHAT HAPPENED

Debbie made snow angels, singing "Frosty the Snowman" over and over again. I made snowballs and threw them at the snowman that Mom and Dad had helped us build a few days before Dad died. The snowman wore Dad's red scarf and three large buttons down his chest. The carrot on the snowman's face was drooping down toward his chin. Suddenly, Debbie jumped up from the snow and hurled a snowball at the snowman, knocking the carrot right off his face.

"Wow. Great shot, Deb!" I laughed.

Someone shouted my name. I turned and saw my neighbor, Brian, walking toward us. Brian was fourteen years old. Although he was three years older than me, we often hung out together. He was one of the tallest kids at school. I wasn't ready to tell him about my dad. In fact, I wanted to stop playing, run into the house, and hide. My heart was beating fast; I was scared to death. When he reached us, Brian gave me a strange look. Did he know about my dad?

"The other day I was home from school because I had a sore throat. I saw two cop cars outside of your house. What happened?"

I didn't want to answer his question, talk about the police or Dad's suicide. But Brian was my friend, so I figured it would be okay to tell him. I had never lied to him. "My dad died while I was at school," I said softly, my hands starting to shake inside my coat pockets.

"Was he in an accident?"

"No. There was no accident," I whispered. It was hard to say— but, I said it, "Nothing like that. My dad died from suicide."

"He killed himself? Aw, man. Why did he do it?"

"I don't know. No one knows for sure. Everyone tells me something different. My mom said he had mental health problems. My aunt said he was in emotional pain. My uncle said something about tunnel vision." Debbie was sucking her thumb. I hadn't realized that she was listening. I hadn't seen her suck her thumb since she was three years old.

In a baby voice she'd outgrown long ago, Debbie told me she wanted to go inside the house. "My tummy feels funny. I want my mommy," she said and ran toward the front door.

"See ya later, Deb," Brian called out.

Talking to Brian about my dad's death wasn't as bad as I thought it would be. My heart was still beating fast, but I felt relieved.

Out of the blue, Brian said, "My cousin Judy died of suicide."

Right then, something clicked in my head. Suicide can happen to anyone. It happens to other kids, too. "Wait, your cousin died, too?"

"Yeah, Judy killed herself last year."

"How old was she?"

"Judy was fifteen."

"Wow. My mom told me that my dad had a problem with his mind. What was your cousin's problem?"

"I don't know. After my cousin died, I heard my uncle Matthew tell my dad that she was doing drugs and sleeping all the time. But no one ever talks to me about her."

"When was the last time you saw her?" I asked.

"The last time I saw her was at a barbeque."

"Did you talk to her?"

Brian kicked at the snow with his boot. "Yeah, just about regular stuff. I had no idea Judy was thinking of killing herself. She died two days later."

"That's really sad."

"She just wasn't herself," said Brian, remembering his last conversation with his cousin. "Even though Judy had always been a good student, she wasn't getting good grades. And she said that she was going to drop out of a club at her school that she really liked. I should have known something was up. Judy told me that she hated her life and that she felt trapped. When we said goodbye, my cousin said that she would text me to meet. She wanted to give me some of her drawings. She told me that she liked to draw pictures of death."

"What kind of drawings?"

"Of dying and heaven."

"Judy was drawing pictures of death? That's weird."

"I didn't get a chance to see them. I didn't realize that the drawings had anything to do with her thinking about killing herself."

"Uh-huh."

"Judy gave me a big hug and whispered, 'You're just better off without me, Brian.' I said, 'Better off? What do you mean?' She told me that she didn't have any hope for the future. I had no idea she was talking about killing herself. I didn't get it. I just told her that everything was going to be okay and that she should speak to her mom or dad. Judy said her parents would just give her advice that doesn't make sense to her."

"Brian, have you talked with your family about what your cousin said to you with your family?"

"Nope. I want to talk about Judy, but every time I bring up her name, someone in my family changes the subject. No one wants to talk about her."

"Maybe they're mad at her."

Brian thought for a moment. "They probably are mad that Judy killed herself. I overheard my uncle say that my cousin had been stealing her mom's medications from the medicine cabinet. But since everyone avoids talking about her with me, I don't know. Maybe they are mad at me, too."

"Why would they be mad at you?"

"Maybe I could have saved her, Alex. Maybe I should have talked to Judy about why she was no longer interested in the things she used to like. Judy said that she felt like a burden. I didn't get into that with her; maybe I should have. I didn't do everything I could have done to save her, and maybe everyone is mad at me for not helping her."

I shrugged my shoulders and said, "Maybe."

"What I *do* know is that I don't want people talking about my cousin only as someone who killed herself," Brian said, his chin jutting out. "My cousin was a great person. Judy loved to dance and listen to music. She always helped me with my math homework. I just don't think she realized how killing herself would hurt me so much."

Brian then said that he was worried about one of his friends. "I have a friend who cuts and scratches her arms. She's not keeping it a secret. She told her parents and goes to a therapist to talk about her feelings. I don't want her to kill herself like my cousin did."

I clenched my hands in my pockets. "I don't like secrets. You're the first friend I've told about what happened to my dad. Is your family keeping your cousin's suicide a secret?"

"No . . . I don't know. It's confusing. No one tells me anything!"

"I'm confused, too, Brian."

"I want to talk about Judy, but no one else in my family wants to."

"Tomorrow's my dad's funeral. Did you go to your cousin's funeral?"

"No, they wouldn't let me. My parents said everyone would be upset and crying at the funeral, and they didn't want me to go through that."

"Did *you* want to go to the funeral?"

"Yeah, I did. Kids aren't allowed to go to funerals in my family. I couldn't go, even though I was already 13 then. I talked to my cousins about it. It's totally unfair! How are we supposed to deal with death if our family doesn't include us? I don't get it."

"My mom asked me if I wanted to go to my dad's funeral. I want to go. She explained everything to me. I know what to expect—the prayers, the eulogy, the casket, the hearse, and the grave."

"The hearse will probably take your dad's body to the cemetery," Brian said.

"Yeah, but I can't believe my dad will be inside a casket," I sighed, as I shook my head.

"Your dad's body will be in the casket. But he's in heaven."

"I know. But, Brian, I'm mad at my dad. I'm mad at God. I'm mad at everyone. Were you mad at God for letting Judy die?"

"No, I wasn't mad at God. I was mad at her for not telling me she was thinking about suicide. When she told me 'it wasn't worth it' and mentioned 'going away,' I thought she was talking about not doing drugs anymore or not going to a club at school or something. I'm not sure what I could have done to save her. But I would have tried to do something if I had known what she was planning to do. I'm mad at her."

I nodded and began kicking at the snow like Brian. "Sometimes I think that God doesn't care about me. Brian, I can't believe this is happening."

"Do you want to come over to my house?" Brian asked.

"Yeah! That's a great idea. Let me tell my mom where I'm going. I'll be right back."

I leaped over a pile of snow, although most of it got inside my boots. I took them off inside the front door and headed for the kitchen.

"There you are," Mom exclaimed. "Sit down. I made buffalo wings." As Mom took out bleu cheese and ranch dressing, she said, "You must be hungry."

"Well, actually, Mom," I interrupted. "I'm still pretty full from breakfast."

"But breakfast was hours ago. And you've been playing in the snow. Debbie told me you were out there talking to Brian. Oh, my goodness, your socks are soaking wet. Take them off."

"But, Mom . . ."

"But, Mom, what? I'd like for you to sit down, warm up, and eat lunch."

"I want to go hang out with Brian."

"Have a quick bite first. Then go. But don't stay late. Tomorrow is Dad's funeral."

After taking off my wet socks, I texted Brian to tell him that I was going to eat and then come over.

Still sucking her thumb, Deb asked, "Is Daddy going to the funeral, too?"

"Daddy is dead, honey. We're all going to Daddy's funeral. Remember, his body will be in a casket," Mom explained again.

"What is Daddy going to do all the time when he's dead?"

"Daddy's body doesn't work anymore. He won't be doing anything. His body will be inside a box and placed in the ground," Mom said with patience.

As I finished my last wing, I lost it. "How many times do you have to tell Debbie the same thing?"

Mom looked at me. "Debbie is not as old as you. It's hard for her to understand what's happening."

"Debbie's five. Why is she sucking her thumb, Mom? Debbie hasn't done that in a long time."

"Debbie is sad that Dad died. Sucking her thumb again makes her feel better. It's her way of coping with his death."

Angrily, I said, "I don't care. I'm sick of talking about coping. I'm sick of talking about Dad's death. I'm sick of listening to you talk about it, Mom. I'm out of here." I started to leave the table.

Firmly, Mom responded, "Wait a minute, Alex. I know you're upset. So am I."

I stopped, suddenly ashamed. My mom had enough to worry about. "I'm sorry, Mom."

"You still need to be respectful."

Now, I really felt bad. "I know. I'm sorry."

Using her baby voice again, Debbie said, "Daddy died. Mommy told me that everybody dies."

"All living things die," Mom said. "Just like the very big elk that we saw on the road the other day. He was alive. Then he got hit by a car and died. We don't know when it's going to happen . . . most people die when they are very old."

"Did Daddy get hit by a car?" Debbie asked.

"No, Daddy took his own life, which made his body stop working."

"Make Daddy come alive again," Debbie demanded.

"Once you're dead, you can't come back to life."

"How long is Daddy going to be dead?"

Mom whispered, "Daddy is going to be dead forever. But I believe even though his body died, his spirit will go to heaven. We talked about this, Deb."

Debbie started to cry. Mom lifted Debbie onto her lap and started to cry, too. They held each other. I heard Debbie whisper, "Why did Daddy leave me?"

"Daddy wasn't thinking right. He loved you very much," Mom reassured her.

Dad's suicide did not make any sense to me. I got up from the table to put on a new pair of socks and go over to Brian's house.

"Mom, I'll be back soon."

"Where are you going?"

"Mom, I already told you. I'm going to hang out with Brian."

"Oh, yeah, right. Before you go, I want to ask you something. I'm going to go through Dad's clothes and pick out a suit for him to be buried in. Do you want to help me pick out his clothes?"

"No, not really."

"You sure?" Mom asked.

I thought for a moment and said, "Mom, he liked his navy suit best."

Mom nodded in agreement. "That's a good choice. Your dad looked handsome in that suit. Thank you for helping me."

On the way to Brian's house, I stopped to read the large sign leaning against our snowman. Only a few days ago, my mom, Dad, Debbie, and I had sung "Frosty the Snowman" and put up the sign which Dad had made from a piece of wood he'd found in the garage. The sign said: "*He waved goodbye, saying don't you cry. I'll be back again someday.*" Those were the last words my dad ever wrote.

Later, I sat in Brian's bedroom, looking up at the poster on the ceiling. It read: "*The difficult we do today. The impossible takes a little longer.*" Brian told me it was the motto of the U.S. Army Corps of Engineers. I thought about Dad again; he had always liked to read quotes to me and then ask me what I thought the quotes meant.

I thought about the times when my dad served in the Army. He had long deployments, but he always came home. Now, he's not coming home. What I was going through was hard. I couldn't imagine anything worse until I thought about tomorrow: my dad's funeral.

Brian took his hamster Marty from the cage and placed him in a small plastic exercise ball on the floor. Marty ran so fast that the ball rolled all around the room. When Marty stopped running, we watched him use his tiny paws to clean his face.

"Can we hold him and feed him some nuts?" I asked.

It's fun to watch Marty eat nuts. He doesn't seem to chew them. Instead, he puts one nut after another in his mouth until his cheeks are full. He tried to stuff one last nut into his mouth, but it wouldn't fit; we laughed so hard that we fell to the floor. Brian almost dropped Marty, but caught him just in time and we burst out laughing again.

Brian said, "Well, I'd say he's full!"

He put Marty back in his cage. We watched the hamster remove each nut from his cheeks by touching both sides of his face. In those few minutes watching Marty, I didn't think of my dad, the funeral, or the snowman sign. I felt a little guilty because I was having fun. I knew my dad would want me to enjoy my life.

Later, on the way home, I stopped and stared at the snowman and the sign. I slowly unwrapped Dad's red scarf from the snowman and took it into the house. I wanted to keep it. I hung my coat in the closet. Mom was sitting on the sofa reading a brochure, "Survive and Thrive," and crying really hard. She reached out her hand to me. I slowly sat down next to her, and she put her arm tightly around me. After a while, my mom stopped crying, and we talked about how it was hard for her to read the brochure because she was so upset. Mom didn't want to hide her feelings from me, she said, because she didn't want me to hide my feelings from her. Mom told me that my grandparents would be arriving soon. They were my dad's parents and they lived far away. I always had fun when they visited. This time would be different.

Ten Years Later

Most of my friends don't know that my dad killed himself. They have both a mom and a dad, and I just want to fit in. A few kids found out from their parents. I just told them that I didn't want to talk about it. I took my dad's desk with me to college. My mom couldn't understand why I wanted that old desk in my dorm room. I couldn't explain it. I just wanted it—just like I wanted his red scarf, which I also brought with me to college. A desk. A scarf. It's amazing how little things can mean so much.

I believe that my dad somehow knows that I'm sitting at his desk or wearing his red scarf. He hears me when I ask him about what he was thinking about before he took his life. Did he only have one plan or was he considering other ways to die? I don't know what could have been that bad that he felt he needed to end his life. Did I miss the warning signs? Was I too young then to understand the mental health issues he was facing? I've been reading about *psychache* in my psychology class. It's when psychological pain is so intense, so intolerable, that people take their own life. Is that what my dad was feeling?

Lori introduced me to her friend Mary from Utah. Mary had been on a Hope Squad in high school, where she had been recognized by her peers as a good listener. Hope Squad students are trained by school counselors and advisors on how to provide friendship and talk to their peers who need help and how to recognize warning signs for suicide.

Mary told me about a student who was upset because he was being bullied. She tried to convince him to speak to an adult in the school, but he refused. She told a school counselor who contacted the student and his parents. He later told Mary that he was going to kill himself. Kids in Mary's high school had looked out for one another. I had no idea that programs like Hope Squad existed, perhaps because I had never thought suicide would become a part of my world.

Last week, a wisdom tooth caused me unbearable pain. I made an emergency appointment with my dentist because the tooth had to be extracted. I know that the extraction would ease my pain. Still, I could not concentrate on anything else. I tried to manage the pain by rinsing my mouth with salt water and putting a cold compress on my cheek. I desperately wanted the pain to stop, but nothing I did helped. Maybe that's how my dad felt. Maybe he had struggled with emotional pain in the same way that I had struggled with physical pain.

Perhaps our brains don't know the difference between emotional and physical pain. Maybe my dad killed himself because he thought his pain would never end. I was in pain and could not imagine living the rest of my life in that much agony. What would I have done if my dentist had been unable to help me? I hope that I would keep reaching out for help. I hope that I would keep searching for someone with the skills to alleviate my pain, someone who has been trained to treat people going through what I was going through, someone with the ability to help me get beyond the pain and back to my life.

Follow-Up Questions

- In what ways can you relate to the family in Chapter 4?

- After the person in your family died, who was the first person with whom you shared what happened?

- What were your feelings when you shared the bad news for the first time?

- Have you ever talked with someone who has had a similar experience?

- If your family believed in heaven and God, did those beliefs help you and, if so, how?

- How difficult has it been for you to move on with life and have fun?

- Alex's personality traits (e.g., empathetic, playful, outgoing) helped him cope with telling a friend what happened. What did you learn about your strengths as you coped with your loss? What strengths helped, or are helping, you cope with the death of your loved one?

CHAPTER 5

Keepsakes and Treasures

Grandma and Grandpa arrived after dinner. We watched TV. After playing a few games on my phone, I went to my room and got into my pajamas. I was tired. Grandma knocked on the door and asked to come in. I was at my desk, flipping through some old comic books.

"That was your dad's desk. I bought it for him a very long time ago," she said, sitting on the edge of my bed.

"Grandma, Dad once told me that he did his homework at this desk when he was a kid."

"It seems like only yesterday that your dad was a boy sitting at that desk." Grandma sighed. "I can't believe he's gone."

I heard Grandpa pacing up and down the hall. Finally, he stopped outside my door, stuck his head into the room, and said, "Hey, Champ." He sounded like Dad. Although it was weird, it felt good—reassuring, almost—to hear Dad's voice. It was something I had always taken for granted—up until now. Grandma told Grandpa to stop pacing. He rolled his eyes and smiled at me.

Stepping into my room, he picked up my magnetic darts and began throwing them at the dart board. He said, "These darts are strong."

"Super strong, Grandpa."

"That's a dangerous toy," Grandma said.

"It's magnetic," Grandpa and I said at the same time.

Sounding worried, she said, "Oh, I just don't want anyone else getting hurt."

Grandpa touched Grandma's shoulder and said, "No one else is going to get hurt, honey." Grandpa looked around my room and noticed my ant farm. "What do you feed your ants?"

"Grandpa, I don't have to feed them. They live in a nutrient gel."

He leaned down and peered into the farm. "Your ants have worked hard creating those long tunnels. There must be at least twenty ants in there." Next to the ant farm was another habitat. "You have hermit crabs, too. You know, your dad liked nature when he was a kid."

Grandma looked sad. She said, "I'm tired. We should all go to bed, including those ants and hermit crabs."

Grandpa mumbled, "I'm sure those ants are tired from digging those tunnels, and those two hermit crabs are tired from lugging their shells around. I'm tired, too. We could all use some sleep."

I started to cry when I heard him say, *We could all use some sleep*, because it was Dad's favorite saying when he was tired.

Realizing why I was sad, Grandma pulled me into her arms. Sitting beside my grandma on my bed, I said, "Grandma, it was strange going to sleep last night."

"Hmm. What was strange about it?"

"It was weird. I kept turning over in my bed, thinking about Dad. I just don't want to have a bad dream."

"Aw," she said. "Bad dreams can be scary. When you were little, you would wake up from a nightmare and tell me that there was a monster in your closet."

But tonight, I wasn't thinking of monsters. I was thinking of my dad and how he really was dead.

Grandma continued, "When I have a bad dream, I imagine ways to change the ending."

"You go back into your bad dream?"

She gave me another squeeze. "Yep. Your grandma is brave. I make the ending one that I like. It's a lot less scary that way. Then I go back to bed."

Grandpa nodded. "Tell him about the time I woke up from a bad dream where a giant was towering over me. You told me to create a magical shield."

"Yep, that giant couldn't hurt Grandpa when he went back into the bad dream because he had a shield to protect him."

"Even though a nightmare is scary, your room is a safe place. And, Alex, God will protect you," Grandpa said, giving me a kiss on the top of my head and leaving the room.

"Grandma, I don't feel safe. Dad is never going to be here to protect me. Uncle Sammy lives thirty minutes away. I was scared last night, but I wasn't thinking about monsters, Grandma."

"What were you thinking about?"

"I was thinking about Dad killing himself. How could God have let that happen?"

Grandma thought for a moment, then said, "Alex, God is with you in your room at night. He will help you to be brave when you're afraid. Just like your night-light that projects stars around the room, God is your personal nightlight. And look at that huge moon," Grandma added, pointing to the window. "God left a light on for you in the sky."

My dad used to say the same thing to me whenever I was scared about something. He must have learned that from Grandma. She paused to glance at all the special stuff in my room: my posters, the photos in frames, my collection of rocks on the dresser. "You sure do have lots of rocks. Look around your room, Alex. All your things are here. Your mom is in her bedroom. Grandpa and I are sleeping over. Debbie is sleeping in your mom's bed. If you have a dream about Dad, good or bad, you can wake me up, and we'll talk about it."

She got up and pulled back the covers of the bed, motioning for me to get in.

"Grandma, I'll try to be as brave as you," I said, sliding between the covers. "Wait a minute. Why is Debbie sleeping in Mom's room?"

"I guess she needs to be close to your mom right now. Sometimes after a death, sleeping in a parent's bed makes very young children feel safe."

As she pulled up the covers around me, I noticed Grandma was wearing a man's watch and asked, "Grandma, are you wearing my dad's watch?"

She touched the watch and talked about how good it felt wearing something that belonged to her son. "Your mom said I could wear it. If you would like it, I can ask your mom if I can give it to you when you are a bit older. Do you want to wear something that belonged to your dad, too?"

Immediately, I said, "I want his favorite T-shirt and his baseball cap."

"I'll be back in a flash," she assured me as she left my room. After a few minutes, she returned and handed me Dad's baseball cap. "Sorry it took so long. Uncle Alan called. He and Aunt Jillian are back at the hotel. He called to make sure you and Debbie were okay." The cap was old and worn, but it was Dad's. It smelled like Dad. As I put it on my head, I thought about him wearing it.

"It's a little bit big for you," Grandma said with a smile, tugging it so it fell down over my eyes.

"I can adjust it," I assured her. It felt good wearing my dad's cap. "Grandma, I like talking to you."

"And I like talking to you, too. It's good to find people to talk to, whether it's someone in your family or a good friend," she said.

"I'm not going to talk with the kids at school about what happened."

"It sounds like you want to keep your dad's death a secret. Why is it that you want to do that?"

"Grandma, the kids at school still have dads. I don't know anyone whose dad killed himself."

She nodded. "That may make it hard for them to understand what you're going through."

"Grandma, they won't get it. I hardly understand it myself."

"Not everyone will understand how much it hurts."

I shrugged and put my head down. "You do, Grandma. But I'm embarrassed." I started to cry so hard I thought I would never stop. I felt the bed move as Grandma sat down again.

"What are you embarrassed about, Alex?" she asked.

"What Dad did was wrong. I don't want anyone to find out," I sobbed.

"There is nothing for you to feel ashamed about. A death by suicide can happen in any family."

"A few years ago, a high school kid in our town killed himself. I didn't know him."

"That's upsetting. Have any of your friends talked about ending their life?"

"No, Grandma."

"If you or anyone you know has thoughts of suicide, always speak to someone. You can always speak with your mom or a teacher. You always have someone to talk to. Also, when someone dies by suicide, or some other disease, it's not going to be easy to talk about it. But there's nothing to be embarrassed about. Like I said, it can happen in any family."

"Grandma, last month, a boy died by a drug overdose. Mom knew his mother. When Mom came home from the funeral, she was sad, and it was hard for her to talk about it but she wanted to make sure I understood how dangerous drugs can be."

Grandma said, "What a tragedy. Adults have a hard time talking about death, no matter what the cause. I imagine it's very hard for you to understand or to put your feelings into words. A death of someone you love is not easy to talk about."

"Talking to you helps a lot, Grandma."

"I'm glad, Alex. Always talk with someone you trust."

"Maybe I'll talk to my teacher about Dad."

"I'm glad you have a teacher to talk with about your feelings."

After giving me the longest hug ever, Grandma stood, and said, "Good night, sleep tight," and she closed my bedroom door. Grandma had tried to help me understand my dad's death. It was hard for Grandma because she did not fully understand it herself. Having my grandparents around was usually comforting, but they seemed different now. I put my dad's baseball cap on the nightstand next to my bed. It had been his, and now it was mine. I thought to myself, if I have a nightmare, I'll put on the baseball cap and it will be my shield.

As I tried to get some sleep, thoughts filled my head. Was Dad now a ghost in my house? Dozing off, I gazed at the stars projected onto the walls and ceiling of my room. Although I would usually stare at them until I fell asleep, I covered my head with my pillow. Shortly after that, I heard a knock at the door and my mom's voice.

"Can I come in?"

"Sure, Mom. I wasn't asleep yet."

"I see you have Dad's baseball cap."

"It's going to protect me while I sleep. It's my shield."

"You've been talking to Grandma, haven't you?"

"Yeah, if I see a ghost in the middle of the night, it will protect me."

"Ghosts are in the movies, Alex, not in real life."

"Dad might be a scary ghost, Mom."

"He is not a scary ghost. Dad is in heaven."

"Are you sure, Mom?"

In a calm, soft voice Mom said, "He is in heaven. That's how I find meaning in Dad's death."

"I know, Mom, but I want him here with me."

With tears in her eyes, Mom whispered, "He *should* be here with you. But remember, no matter where Dad is, he will always be a part of you."

"He's dead, Mom." I didn't want to talk about it anymore. "I'm tired."

"Me, too."

"Good night, Mom."

"It's been a long day, and tomorrow is going to be just as long. Tomorrow is Dad's funeral. We're going to get up early. Try to get some sleep. I love you."

I picked up the night-light, and together we watched the stars dance around the room until I finally drifted off to sleep.

Ten Years Later

Going back to school after my dad died wasn't as big of a deal as I feared it would be. The first day back at school, I couldn't stop wondering if my friends were talking about me. I had trouble focusing. During the first few weeks, my teachers let me leave the classroom anytime I needed to, when I felt down and couldn't concentrate. Thankfully, no one at school said anything stupid. No one asked me how he died or why he did it. Two friends did say they were sorry my dad died and, eventually, I made new friends who didn't know my dad had died by suicide. At that time in my life, I just wanted to fit in and be normal like everyone else.

Most people didn't get it. How could they? Nearly everyone I knew had both a mom and a dad who were alive. There were times when I wished my friends had asked me about my feelings. We talked about school and sports, but never about how I was feeling since Dad died. If they had asked, I would have opened up to them.

Some school events really made me miss Dad. Mom and I had fun at *Muffins with Mom Day*. But I didn't go to school on *Doughnuts with Dad Day*, even though Uncle Sammy offered to go with me.

There were many reminders of Dad around us: his clothes, his tools, the things he kept in his pockets or lying around the house. Mom told me that even though Dad was dead, we could keep things that reminded us of him. She donated some of Dad's things to charity; others went to Debbie, Grandma, Grandpa, or my uncles. Before giving away something that had belonged to my dad, Mom would always ask me whether I wanted it.

One day she found Dad's electric shaver and asked me if I wanted it. I didn't need it yet but she realized that sooner or later I would. I felt a jolt when I heard the sound of my dad's razor. Then I got sad. Seeing the razor reminded me that my dad would never teach me how to shave. I knew the sound because my dad had used it every day. Occasionally, he would chase me around the house, laughing and pretending he was going to give me a shave. Mom handed the shaver to me and told me to keep it for the time when I got my "peach fuzz." She tried to make me smile, but we both knew that this would have been Dad territory.

As I look back at how Mom handled my dad's death during that first year, I realize that although she was falling apart, she was always there for me and Debbie, talking about Dad and helping us remain connected to him.

There are certain times when I miss my dad the most. I usually talk to him while I'm driving. Mom gave me Dad's car keys on the day I passed my driver's test. It was a big day in my life. Mom did a good job teaching me how to drive. But I think my dad would have really liked taking on that job.

I sometimes dream about Dad and the way things were when he was alive. It feels real. I like to believe that these dreams are his special way of communicating with me. Every night, I look out of my dorm window and pray. Once I'm finished talking to God, I save time for Dad. I still talk to his photograph. He can hear me. It feels good, like a relief; so why not talk to him? Grandpa once said to me, "When your dad starts answering you back, then you've got issues. Until then, keep talking."

- In what ways can you relate to the family in Chapter 5?

- Has anyone ever said or done something that reminded you of the person who died? If so, explain what it was.

- If you believe that there are certain people with whom you should not share your loss, how does that belief keep you safe?

- Have you had any dreams about the person who died? If so, describe your dreams.

- Is there a physical place where you feel safest?

- Is there a special person with whom you feel safest?

- If you believe in a higher power, how does that belief help you deal with your loss?

- If you could have one item that belonged to the person who died, what would it be?

- If you already have something that belonged to this person, describe it and its special meaning.

- If you have felt embarrassed about the cause of your loved one's death, how did you manage your feelings?

- Do you communicate with your deceased loved one?

- Alex's personality traits (e.g., brave, loving, thoughtful) helped him cope when he did not feel safe. How do you put your strengths into practice to cope with your painful loss?

CHAPTER 6

A Bereaved Family

If I were to ask you what day was the saddest day in your life, what day would you choose? For me, it was my dad's funeral. I couldn't take my eyes off the casket. Once I saw the large hole with dirt all around it, I started to cry. The casket was going to be lowered into the ground, and I would never see my dad again. Uncle Sammy gave the eulogy. Grandma and Grandpa were holding each other. My mom didn't say anything. She cried the entire time. Everything felt gloomy, and no one was smiling.

Someone played "Taps" on a bugle and then two army soldiers removed the American flag that was on Dad's casket, folded it, and gave it to Mom. Aunt Jillian held Debbie's hand as Debbie held onto her doll, and I just tried to be brave. I could hear my dad in my head calling me "Champ" and telling me to "hang in there." It sounded real, like he was there with me. But I honestly didn't even know how I should feel. My dad was dead.

Someone said a final prayer, and it was over. As I walked back to the car, Dad's boss told me that my dad was a good man. His friend told me that he would miss him. Another lady from his office told me how sorry she was that he died. I told her that I had placed a few rocks in the casket along with a photograph of us fishing and that Debbie had drawn a picture for Dad to put in the casket. The lady said that was a nice way to say goodbye.

It was a cold day, and there were lots of people standing around my dad's grave. The service went really fast. At one point, only Debbie, my mom, and I were left at the grave. My mom held Debbie's hand as they both said goodbye to my dad for the last time. Then Mom told me that she and Debbie would wait for me in the car.

As I stood at my dad's grave, I told him everything I needed to say. I told him how much I missed him. He had been dead only a couple of days. I had no idea at the time that missing him would be something I would have to live with for the rest of my life.

Lots of people came back to our house after the funeral. Debbie started once again singing "Frosty the Snowman." She kept singing the song over and over again. Usually, Debbie's singing and playing at the table didn't bother me. Today, for some reason, I couldn't stand it.

A week before Dad died, Debbie had had a birthday party. She got dolls and coloring books. Her Barbie cake had pink and purple icing and five magic candles that she couldn't blow out. Dad grabbed the spray bottle filled with water that Mom used on her plants and sprayed the candles. He then sprayed Debbie, and we all laughed so hard. I'm trying to remember my dad like that. But I'm angry that he left me.

"Deb, stop singing," I pleaded, but she kept getting louder and louder. "I can't hear myself think!"

Mom dropped her fork and stared at me. Dad used to say that.

I guess it reminded both Mom and Debbie of Dad because Debbie then asked, "Where's Daddy?"

Mom whispered, "Debbie, remember we talked about Daddy. He's dead, sweetheart. We went to his funeral today. Daddy died."

"Daddy died?" Debbie asked.

"Yes, Deb, he's in heaven," my mother reassured her.

"Did a monster take him, Mommy?" Debbie asked.

"Don't be stupid, Debbie," I shouted.

Mom shot me a look and then explained once again, "Debbie, there's no such thing as a monster."

Debbie dropped her crayons, "If I wish really hard, could I make Daddy come back?"

If it were only that easy, I thought. Mom said no.

But Debbie wouldn't let it go. "I wish Daddy was home. What time is he coming home?"

I tried to ignore Debbie, but she didn't get it. It was hard to keep in mind that she was little. I felt that I should explain things to her because I'm her big brother and I'm supposed to know the answers.

"Daddy's never coming home," I said. "No monster harmed him. We don't have the power to wish him back home, or back with us at the kitchen table. He's going to be dead forever."

"Forever?" she asked.

As I explained, the truth started to sink in for me. Dad was never coming home. Our breakfast, or any meal, would never be the same. No matter what time of day it was, or what meal we ate together, he would never sit with us at the kitchen table ever again.

Holding Debbie's hand, Mom said, "Deb, when people die, their bodies don't work anymore. Daddy's body doesn't work anymore."

"Daddy's body doesn't work?" Debbie asked.

"No, it doesn't. His heart stopped beating. He doesn't breathe anymore."

"How can Daddy eat if he can't breathe?" Debbie asked.

"He can't eat, honey. When people are dead, they don't need to eat."

"Daddy loves hot dogs. Doesn't he want to eat a hot dog while he's in heaven?" Debbie asked.

"He can't eat anymore because his body doesn't work. He's at peace. He doesn't need food like we do."

After Mom told Debbie that our dad was dead for what felt like the hundredth time, she told Mom that her tummy hurt. While gently rubbing Debbie's stomach, Mom expressed how sad we all felt because Dad was dead. "Although it's all a mystery that we don't understand, I believe Dad is in heaven."

Suddenly, I had a terrible thought. Panicked, I asked, "Mom, what if you die?"

Mom replied reassuringly, "That's a very scary question, Alex. But I am healthy and I want to live," Mom said.

"Grandma and Grandpa are old. They could die."

Mom spoke in her sweetest voice. It was the voice she used when she knew I was scared about something. "You're right; they could die. We are all going to die one day. Lucky for us, Grandma and Grandpa are both healthy. You needn't worry about that right now."

"I'm going to draw a picture of Daddy in heaven," Debbie vowed.

"Show me . . . I want to see it when you're done," I said, pouring a glass of orange juice.

I turned to Mom. "Mom, do you believe that Dad can see us from heaven?"

"Dad does not watch us all the time," she said. "But he can see us when we need him to see us."

"What's heaven like, Mom?" I asked.

"It's peaceful. Love exists in heaven. Dad is with all the angels. He's with our family and friends who have died. And when we need to feel his presence, he'll be smiling down on us from heaven."

Debbie looked at me. "God is in heaven. Daddy is with God," she said.

Mom smiled and said, "In some ways, that thought is getting me through this hard time. I believe Dad's no longer hurting inside. Heaven is filled with sunlight. It's peaceful." Mom glanced out the kitchen window and up at the clouds. Without taking her eyes off the sky, Mom asked, "What do you suppose heaven is like, Alex?"

"Mom, heaven is a place where people don't hurt. It's a place where we see people who have died, even cats. When Jaxson died, Dad told me that our cat was in heaven."

As my mom kept staring at the sky, tears began to roll down her cheeks. I heard her whisper, "Oh, how I miss that cat. I remember how I cried when he died." As we spoke, people were coming in and out of the kitchen. Mom's friend Chris came over and put her arms around Mom before walking back into the living room to join all of the other people who had gathered at the house after the funeral.

"Mom, don't you remember what Grandpa told us after his dog died? He said that he would see Patches again one day in heaven."

Grandma overheard us as she walked into the kitchen. She said, "I recently saw a poster of cats with a saying underneath that read: 'Heaven is where all the cats we ever loved will meet us once again.'" Grandma poured coffee into a cup. On one side of the cup were the words, "Best Dad in the Whole World."

"I guess heaven is filled with old friends, family, cats, and dogs," Mom sighed.

"Birds, too, Mommy. They fly right up there," Debbie squeaked.

When I realized what cup Grandma was using, I shouted, "That's Dad's coffee cup, Grandma! You're drinking from his cup. That's . . ."

Grandma looked more closely at the cup. "My goodness. I'm sorry. I didn't realize it was Bill's cup."

Mom assured Grandma, "It's fine. You can use Bill's cup."

Still, Grandma hesitated, "Do you mind if I use your dad's cup, Alex?"

"I don't mind. It's just, well, it's Dad's cup."

Grandma started pouring out the coffee. "I can see how you feel about your dad's cup. I can use another one."

"No, Grandma, use it. Dad would probably say it's okay, too. He's not here, so we can't ask him."

Grandma refilled the cup and sat down next to me. "I wonder if Dad can hear us talking," I thought out loud.

Mom suggested, "When you have something to say that you want Dad to hear, he will be able to hear you. What do you want to say to him?"

"I would ask him why he killed himself."

"And how would Dad answer you?" Mom asked.

"Maybe he would say he was sorry . . . He would say that he should have stayed alive to be with me. I'm mad that he killed himself. Now, he won't be here to take me places and spend time with me. I understand he's with God, but I want him with me."

"It's not fair," Mom said. She picked up a book that had been lying on the table and showed it to me. It was full of blank pages. She handed it to me and suggested that a journal might be a good place to start writing about my thoughts and feelings. I thanked her and decided I wanted to be alone in my room. I walked through the living room. I didn't know half the people standing around the room.

In my room, I stared at the journal for a while, then placed it on the shelf right between my two favorite books about magic and mysteries. It was hard to concentrate. There were many people in the house. I walked back into the kitchen and noticed Mom was talking to Grandma. I wondered what Mom was going to do with Dad's cup. It was weird seeing Grandma drinking from it.

Our next-door neighbors came in and hung up their heavy coats in the hall closet. As they moved a few coats around, I saw it . . . Dad's blue coat. I couldn't move. I just stared at his coat. In that moment, I just wanted to hold onto the coat and make believe he was in it. They closed the closet door, and I still stood there, staring at the door. I felt like I couldn't move. Mom saw that I was getting upset and walked over to me.

"You okay?" she asked. I slowly shook my head. We sat down on the sofa near the warm fireplace. I told her about Dad's coat and she started to cry. Sitting there with her, I was reminded of the many times my dad and I had sat in this very same spot roasting marshmallows in the fire.

"Mom, who lit the fireplace?"

"I did. There's a first time for everything, Alex. I have a feeling there will be a lot of firsts around here. How are you feeling, sweetie?"

Although the room was warm, I suddenly felt cold. I felt . . . Ugh, I didn't know how I felt.

"I feel weird. I'm shaky."

"When someone we love dies, our body reacts."

"My chest feels tight, Mom. I feel like I've forgotten how to breathe."

"Do you remember when I was talking with Debbie a little while ago about Dad's death and she complained about her tummy hurting?"

"Yeah, I remember."

"It's normal to have a stomachache. Certain thoughts, feelings, and behaviors will change as you grieve. I've had a nonstop headache these past few days and it's perfectly normal. It's called grief. It is when our body and mind try to handle a loss. We are having grief reactions because Dad died."

"I'm really sad and really mad, Mom."

Mom put her arm around me. "I know. I feel like I can't stop crying. Sometimes I get mad, too. Whenever that happens, I try to recall a happy memory of your dad and me together."

"I can't cry in front of the kids at school. They'll think I'm weird." Just thinking about school upset me.

"Sounds like crying in front of the other kids could be overwhelming."

"If the kids see me cry, they might start laughing and tease me, call me a baby."

"They might. That's because they don't understand, not because there's anything wrong with crying when someone we love dies," she explained.

"If they tease me, can I hit them?"

"Fighting with other kids isn't going to solve your problem. Try not to act on your angry feelings."

I sighed. "Okay, Mom."

"Grief doesn't give you the right to harm people with your words or actions. Instead of hitting someone, is there something else you can do if you're angry at school?"

I thought for a moment. "I could walk away from the kids who tease me."

"That's a good idea. What else could you do?"

"I could tell a teacher."

"I like your ideas. I don't want to have to worry about your getting into a fight. Just ignore the kids who tease you and realize that they are not kind people."

"Don't worry, Mom," I reassured her. Then another thought came into my head. "I guess I could play sports. That always helps me get out my anger. I'm mad Dad's dead. Why did he want to leave us? Why did he want to leave me?"

"He didn't want to leave you . . . He wanted to end his pain. I'm just trying to figure out what had caused his painful feelings. Dad worried all the time. He couldn't concentrate. He didn't want to talk about his feelings. Wow . . . this is hard. I need one of your hugs, sweetie." I felt numb as we hugged each other. Mom promised, "We are a family, and as a family, we will get through all of this together. Okay?"

"Mom, lately Dad didn't want to play ball with me. I was confused because he'd always played ball with me."

"Lately, your dad hadn't had an interest in anything."

"Not even me, Mom, not even me."

"He was always interested in you. Your dad loved you. I just don't know what he had been thinking."

I felt my face get hot. "He wasn't thinking of me. He should have come to me, Mom."

Mom whispered, "He should have reached out for help. We would have made sure he'd be okay."

Mom was talking about how Dad hadn't been able to solve his problems. He should have chosen to get help. That's when I stopped listening and sat frozen on the sofa. I stared out the window at the trees covered in snow. I had a million thoughts in my head. Why did he kill himself? How could he do this to me? Who is going to help me with my homework? What am I going to tell my friends? Should I still be in the school play? Who is going to take me to baseball practice? Is Mom going to kill herself? I couldn't speak. I thought and thought and thought until my head started to ache. I went into my bedroom and stayed there for a long time. When I returned to the kitchen, I sat down and stared into space. Mom tried to get my attention.

Mom suggested, "Let's go back to what you said before."

I didn't answer and felt like I was miles away. Mom asked, "Are you listening to me as I'm talking to you? Is there something about Dad that's on your mind right now? You can talk to me. I want you to talk to me."

"Mom, maybe if I had been with Dad, I could have kept him alive."

"There wasn't anything you could have done."

"I was his son. I should have known he was going to kill himself. I should never have gone to school the day Dad died."

"Had Dad told you that he was going to kill himself?" Mom asked.

"No, but—"

"But what?" Mom interrupted. "Could you read his mind? I know that I couldn't. Neither could his doctor, and he's trained to see the signs."

All I knew was Dad was dead and that I had never felt this bad in my life. "Mom, it's unfair. I want my dad."

Before long, most of the people in the house went home. I went to my room and tried to sleep and not think about my dad killing himself. I held my pillow and cried so hard that I thought I would never stop.

Ten Years Later

My birthday was hard that first year. How could I celebrate my birthday without my dad? Mom gave me a telescope. On the card she wrote, Love, Mom and Dad. I knew he was in heaven, but seeing the word *Dad* on the card made me feel close to him. At times I felt that he was watching over me when I needed him—like a special guardian angel.

I especially felt that way on Dad's birthday and on Father's Day. Those two days were always special for me. Mom made my dad's favorite strawberry shortcake, loaded with strawberries, on both his birthday and Father's Day. I used to make my dad a special card for both his birthday and Father's Day. After the last bite of cake, we would turn our attentions to the cards and gifts. Even now, twice a year, I still make sure that I eat a piece of strawberry shortcake in Dad's memory.

Debbie just celebrated her birthday. Although she is a teenager, she wanted a Barbie birthday cake with pink and purple icing and magic candles that she would not be able to blow out. Mom said it looked exactly like the cake Debbie had when she was five years old. I remember how Dad grabbed the spray bottle filled with water and sprayed the candles and Debbie. That was the last birthday he celebrated with us.

As we ate the cake, we talked about Dad. Mom said that a few weeks ago, she and my grandma went to a half-day suicide loss survivor workshop. It helped her to be with people whose loved ones had died by suicide. Although I didn't go with her to the workshop, I did participate in the Out of the Darkness Walk the last time I was home. It was a day for us to honor Dad, to walk with hundreds of people—some dealing with the suicide of a loved one, some who just wanted to support the cause of suicide awareness.

This was our third time doing the Out of the Darkness Walk. Lots of people wore T-shirts with pictures of their loved ones who had killed themselves. I always wear my dad's baseball cap for the walk. I walk for my dad, and for all the other survivors who struggle with their loss. Mom said that by going on the community walk, we raise awareness of suicide and help to prevent it.

It's amazing how my mom comforts others during the Walk. I know how hard my dad's death has been for her, yet I see her hugging people she doesn't even know. The Walk reminds Mom that she is not alone. I read a few of the flyers about suicide at the last Out of the Darkness Walk. I learned that there are an average of 129 suicides each day. That's just a staggering fact.

Follow-Up Questions

- In what ways can you relate to the family in Chapter 6?

- If you attended the funeral of your loved one, describe what you saw.

- If you had to explain death to someone younger than yourself, what would you say?

- Were you ever afraid that someone else you cared about was going to die? If so, please explain.

- If you see items that belonged to the person who died, how does that make you feel?

- If you could say anything you wanted to the person who died and that person could hear you, what would you say?

- If you felt angry after your loved one died, what did you do to deal with your feelings?

- Has someone assumed responsibilities around the house that used to be handled by your loved one?

- What grief reactions have you noticed in your body?

- Does your belief about the afterlife give you a sense of hope?

- Alex's personality traits (e.g., careful, assertive, self-controlled) helped him cope with his painful grief process. How did you put your strengths into practice to manage one of the saddest days in your life?

CHAPTER 7

Positive Relationships

Two days after the funeral, Aunt Jillian and Uncle Alan went back to Las Vegas, and Uncle Sammy went back to work. Grandma and Grandpa planned to stay at our house for a few weeks. Debbie and I were taking the remainder of the week off from school. My report on Thomas Jefferson was due today. My science project on the galaxy was due in a few days. I thought about working on the science project, but my stomach began to growl. It was lunchtime. I went to the kitchen and rummaged through the cabinets. Which flavor of cookie did I want—chocolate chip or oatmeal raisin? As I was trying to decide, the doorbell rang.

"Can you get the door?" asked Mom, who was standing at the kitchen counter talking on the phone.

It was my baseball coach Andy, and he'd brought pizza. He must have just gotten back from vacation. He had chapped lips, and his face was as red as a watermelon.

"Boy, do you have a sunburn, Coach!"

"Yeah, I know. You'd never know I'd used sunscreen, huh? It was hot in Florida," he chuckled.

"Come on in. Did you have fun, Coach?"

"I did. Thanks for asking."

Coach stepped into the foyer, and I closed the front door behind him. Then he turned to me and said, "When I got back, I heard the news that your dad died. I'm sorry, Alex."

"Thanks, Coach."

He handed me the pizza box and said with a grin, "I snuck out of school to bring you a pizza. I have to tell ya, kid, I don't have a pass."

"You don't need one, Coach."

"Oh, right! I forgot." As we stood in the foyer laughing, I realized that I needed to laugh. For that moment, I felt like my life was normal. It felt good, but suddenly, I started to feel guilty, too. My dad had died, and here I was laughing. I didn't like the way I felt. My stomach growled. Pointing to my belly, Coach, asked, "Is there a bear cub in there?"

"Yeah, he's hibernating, Coach."

Mom got off the phone and poked her head out from the kitchen, "Andy, thanks for calling me this morning and coming by— and bringing pizza. Please, come in and eat." While Mom poured our drinks and set the table, Coach told her how sorry he was about my dad's death. Mom thanked him, as she opened the box of pizza and handed both of us a paper plate. "Dig in! If you'll excuse me, I have to make a few more phone calls." Mom walked up the stairs, leaving me and Coach alone.

"Hey, kid, why does a round pizza come in a square box?" Coach asked.

"I have no idea. Wait. Coach, I have one. What do you call a deer with no eyes?"

"What?"

"No Eye Deer."

After a few bites of pizza, I asked a question that had been on my mind. Since Dad had always taken me to baseball practice, I was afraid I might not be part of the team anymore. "My dad always took me to the games. Who's going to take me to my practice and games now?"

Coach suddenly leaned forward, put his elbows on the kitchen table, and looked intently at me. "If your mom gives me her permission, I can take you. Would you like that?"

"Yeah. Thanks, Coach."

I closed my eyes for a couple of seconds and thought about the times Dad was in the stands, cheering me on. It was hard for me to believe that he would not be there now. "I still can't believe my dad won't be at my games anymore . . ."

"I can tell something else is bothering you. Tell me what is on your mind," said Coach.

"I'm thinking about the last time I saw my dad."

"Where was he?"

"He was at this table. He took the day off from work. He usually drank coffee and read the paper. That morning, he wasn't doing either one. I should have known something was wrong."

"It sounds like you're blaming yourself."

"I didn't get the chance to say goodbye to my dad."

"Did he say goodbye to you?"

"No." I could feel the tears rising inside me. "Coach, I was late for the bus and ran out of the house."

"Sounds like you're upset with yourself for not saying goodbye to him."

"Coach, I wish I had said goodbye."

"You can always say goodbye."

"No way, Coach. Dad is dead. It's too late to say goodbye."

"You could write your dad a goodbye letter," he suggested.

"I don't know what I would say."

"Write down whatever it is you need to say to him. You can keep that letter in a special place."

"I'm fuming inside. He killed himself, and I never got the chance to say goodbye."

"I believe when someone we care about dies, we have to say goodbye little by little to the things we shared with them. On the other hand, your dad will always be a part of you."

I whispered, "But I didn't say goodbye."

Very slowly, Coach repeated himself, "You can always say good-bye. There are ways to say goodbye to your dad. You can speak to him in the quiet of your room or when you visit the cemetery."

"I just can't believe he's dead. He won't be at any more of my games."

"Try to remember the good times you shared with your dad. Remember when we won last year's season opener? Your dad jumped up and down and fell over. He didn't hurt himself but boy, that was funny."

The memory made me smile. "Yeah, that was hysterical. I never saw my dad so happy. He was taking videos with his cell phone in one hand and holding a hot dog in the other."

"Good memories, kid. That's what you have to hold onto. When my dad died a few years ago, I made a list of all my favorite memories of him. I still have that list."

"Your dad died, too?"

"Yeah. And do you know what? I still miss him to this day."

"Everything has changed."

We finished our last bites of pizza. Coach said, "Some things will change, but a lot of things will be the same as they always were. You will still go to school . . . still read books you enjoy . . . still play baseball . . . and still have your friends on the team."

"I guess. Coach, I don't want to tell anyone on my team that my dad died."

"Why not?"

Hunched over my empty plate, I said, "I don't know what they would say. I'm embarrassed."

"Embarrassed about what?"

"About my dad having killed himself."

"Is there a reason for you to feel shame?"

"He left me. I don't want to feel judged because my dad died."

Coach placed another slice of pizza on my plate and his. I didn't look at Coach. I didn't want to look at anyone. Slumping down into the chair, I said, "When I get to school, I'll just pretend it never happened. I'm going to keep it a secret."

Coach's voice was confident. "You'll figure it out. Personally, I don't think there should be any stigma around suicide. Your dad must have been in so much pain to do what he did."

"I'm nervous. What should I say if someone on my team finds out that my dad killed himself and asks me why he did it?"

"I can see how that might worry you. The question 'why?' is a difficult question to answer. You are just learning the 'whys' yourself. Share what you know, but only if you want to."

"No," I said loudly, pushing my plate away. "If anyone finds out my dad died and stares at me or laughs at me, I'm going to get really mad. I hate being teased."

"I can see where that might make you feel uncomfortable. A kid at school might stare at you or avoid you. Someone may say they're sorry your dad died. Keep thinking positive. Stick with your good friends."

"I don't want to be treated differently. I don't want them to act weird or anything."

"How do you think they'll act?"

"I don't know. I don't want to get sad around anyone at school. Most of all, I don't want anyone to see me cry. They would just call me a baby or something."

"Who can you reach out to at school if you get upset?"

"I guess I can talk with my teacher."

"That's a good way to protect yourself. And you can find me and talk to me as well. I'll be there for you."

"Thanks, Coach."

Coach patted my shoulder. "Has anyone you've known died before?"

"No, not a person. My cat, Jaxson, died last year, and my grandpa's dog, Patches, died, too."

"It's sad when a pet dies. Tell me more about how you felt when Jaxson died."

"I blamed myself. I thought I could have done something to keep him alive. I cried a lot. I miss him. The day he died, my friend, Toby, asked me to come to his house for lunch. I told him I wasn't hungry even though I was. He had a cat, Aly, and I didn't feel like seeing his cat."

"Aly Cat . . . What would have happened if you had gone to Toby's house?"

"Aly would have rubbed against my leg just like Jaxson used to do. It would have been hard to play with Aly when I was upset about my own cat dying."

"Did you ever go back to Toby's house?"

"Yeah, after a couple of weeks I went back to Toby's house and when I returned home, I took a picture of Jaxson out of an album and put it in a frame on my bulletin board. I kept his stuffed mouse, the one I used to dip with catnip. He'd swat at it and it would sail through the air. Sometimes, it even hit the ceiling."

"You have some happy memories of Jaxson."

"I guess I do. All I know for sure is that I still miss him. And now, I miss my dad, too."

Talking to someone I trusted made me feel better. Coach didn't have all the answers, but it felt good knowing that he was trying to understand how I felt. He told me that he had to get back to school or he would get suspended. I walked with him to the front door. As he headed toward his truck, he turned back and said with a grin, "If I don't hurry, the principal will probably make me clean the school, too."

I grinned back because I knew that was what he wanted me to do—feel better. As I was closing the door, he said, "Oh, wait one minute. I almost forgot. I'll be right back." He quickly ran to his truck and came back to hand me a book about baseball. "Whenever I'm feeling gloomy, I read books about things I enjoy doing. I thought this might help you out, Alex."

"Thanks, Coach. And thanks for the pizza."

"Like I said, if you ever need someone to talk to, I'm here for you."

When Coach left, I went to my room and sat at my desk, which was littered with schoolbooks, a test paper my mom had to sign, an empty can of soda, and two dead batteries. "Why do people have to die?" I said, as I threw the batteries into the wastebasket. Looking at my desk, I wondered whether my dad had kept his papers and pens in the same drawer as I did when the desk was his. My dad had told me that he kept his gyroscope and string in the bottom drawer. I always keep mine on the shelf. As I removed my gyroscope and string from the shelf and put them in a box in the bottom drawer, I thought about what my dad had once said about the gyroscope: no matter what direction the gyroscope goes, it always rights itself and keeps on spinning.

Ten Years Later

Last week, I found my gyroscope, hidden behind some old textbooks in the bottom drawer of my desk. I took it out of the box and put the string through the hole just the way my dad had taught me. I wrapped most of the string tightly around the middle bar and with the remaining end wound tightly around my finger, I pulled the string away. I then placed the string on the table and put the gyroscope on top of the string. And just like my dad used to do, I picked up both ends of the string and the gyroscope balanced in the air.

After a couple of minutes, I decided to do my dad's trick. I wrapped the string around my finger, pulled, placed the gyroscope back in its box, and watched as the box spun around. My dad used to say that no matter what direction you are pulled in, be like a gyroscope. Stay balanced. He had said that the force that keeps the gyroscope going is a mystery. As long as the wheel keeps spinning, it will not fall over or drop. I wondered if he was trying to tell me something.

It feels like yesterday . . . playing with the gyroscope with Dad or having pizza with my coach Andy after my dad died. I am thankful to my mom for letting my coach become a big part of my life. It didn't occur to me until recently how much impact Coach has had on my life. I confided in Andy a lot and still text him whenever I get a chance, even though I'm in college now. When he took me to the games, it helped to distract me from my grief. That was important for me, just as important as sharing my grief.

Coach kept his word. He drove me to each practice and game, but every time I looked up into the stands, I was reminded that my dad was dead. Mom, Deb, and Uncle Sammy were always there, smiling and cheering for me. I would smile and wave at them. Still, I missed my dad. I still have a great relationship with Andy, and my mom considers him to be a role model. I always tried my best to win. And when the team lost, I treated the other team with respect. That's what my dad had taught me. Coach helped me build self-reliance. Although I knew Coach would be there for me, I didn't have my dad anymore and I felt that I needed to be resourceful. During those years, I struggled to figure it all out while managing some painful feelings.

Having Andy in my life made me realize how important it was to have someone older to look up to. For that reason, I made sure I talked with Debbie about Dad and tried my best to answer her questions, which changed as she got older. When Dad died, Debbie didn't understand suicide. For that matter, I didn't either. But as a 5-year-old, Debbie didn't even understand death. I wanted to be strong for her and probably didn't show her how much I was hurting.

Now, Debbie is 15. I'm still there for her. Because she doesn't remember our dad like I do, I share my memories of him with her. I wonder what it will be like next year when Dad is not at Debbie's sweet sixteen party, or later on when he's not at her high school graduation. I can't even imagine what it will be like for Debbie when she walks down the aisle on her wedding day and doesn't have our dad by her side.

Follow-Up Questions

- In what ways can you relate to the family in Chapter 7?

- Are you making any plans to do things that you once enjoyed doing with your loved one?

- Did the person who died do things for you that another person is now doing?

- Write a list of comments that people made after the death that you found to be helpful.

- What were some comments people made after the death that made you feel worse, or more confused or angry instead of better?

- What was your biggest fear after this person died?

- How did you cope with your fear?

- Write down some of your good memories of your loved one.

- Alex's personality traits (e.g., humorous, hopeful) helped him focus on positive relationships in his life. How did you use your strengths to maintain positive relationships with others?

CHAPTER 8

A Children's Grief Support Center

As I walked into the kitchen to get some chocolate milk, Mom was seated at the kitchen table, talking on the phone to someone. "It's been one month. Where did the time go? I can't believe Bill has been gone a whole month . . . I can't accept that Bill killed himself . . . I've been robbed of a husband . . . a father for my kids . . . I'm finding it hard to function, Chris . . . Yeah, I'll call the therapist you mentioned. Maybe she can help . . . I'll call, but it's hard for me to plan anything right now. Of course, I'm bitter . . . I know . . . I know . . . I'll let you know."

Mom hung up the phone. When she looked up and saw me, she explained, "That was my friend Chris. She gave me the number of a therapist she went to a few years ago."

"Will I have to go?"

"No, you won't have to go. The therapist is for me. But, I'll talk to her about our family. She may want to meet you and Debbie. I'm not sure. It's hard being bereaved."

"Huh?"

"Bereaved means that we experienced a big loss when Dad died. My heart broke when he died. I'm having a really hard time handling it, Alex."

I went over to her and stood beside her chair. "You're fine, Mom."

"I'm trying my best. But I feel so disorganized, and I'm exhausted." Mom sighed, rubbing her hands across her face. "I'm trying to read this book about coping after a suicide. Most people do fine without profes- sional help, they don't need to see a therapist. But I think I do need to speak to someone. I lost Dad in such a terrible way."

"I know, Mom."

Without hesitating, Mom added, "I need help, Alex. I'm anxious, my thoughts are racing, and I'm shaky. I just can't stop thinking about what happened; it runs over and over again in my mind. I just can't stop it."

I placed my hand on her shoulder. "I'll help you, Mom."

She tried to smile at me. "You are such a big help. I'm just tired. My body is exhausted. Remember we talked about how our bodies react to loss?"

"I had a bad headache the other day, Mom."

"And that's normal."

"Yeah, but why would you want to talk to a stranger about your feelings, Mom?"

"Grief hurts," Mom continued, "Most people don't need to see a therapist. They have friends, relatives, or their faith to help them when their grief becomes painful."

I sat down at the table. "You have those things, Mom."

"Yes, I do. But I need more. What happened to all of us was very traumatic. I want to make sure you and Debbie are okay, and that I'm doing the right things to help you."

"We're okay, Mom."

"A few days ago, Debbie woke up screaming in the middle of the night. I couldn't console her. I need to talk to a therapist about your sister. I don't know what to do. I'll go once and see if therapy is for me."

"If Debbie needs help, I guess you should go," I said. "Mom, I wish we could go back to the way we were before Dad died."

"Me, too. I'm still in shock, even now a month later. I can't accept that Dad is dead. I'm numb."

"Me too, Mom."

"I keep telling myself that this just can't be true. I'm preoccupied with Dad. I can't think of anything else."

"Yeah, me too, Mom."

"That's the way it is when someone we love dies. I feel empty inside. What about you? What are you feeling?"

I didn't have to think long about her question. The answer just spilled out. "Mom, I'm really mad, and very confused."

"Me, too. I'm going to a bereavement support group in a couple of weeks. It's called SOLAS, which stands for Sharing Our Loss After Suicide. The group is for adults and meets at a grief support center."

"A support group?"

"Yeah, a group of people who offer support to others who have lost a loved one and are having trouble handling it. I spoke with the facilitator. She told me that each person in the group lost someone they cared about to suicide. They meet once a month to talk about their feelings—"

I interrupted, "Mom, do you really want to talk about Dad with a group of people you don't know?"

"They'll probably talk about their loved ones, too."

Mom told me that she was going to look into a children's bereavement support group for Debbie and me. I did not want to go.

"Forget it, Mom. I'm not going to a support group."

"All the kids in the group will be just like you. They have had someone they care about die."

"I don't care. I'm not going . . ."

Mom thought it was a good idea for me to check it out. She promised that if I didn't like it, I would never have to go back. Two weeks later, Mom, Debbie, and I took a tour of the place where the support group meets. I hadn't known what to expect. It wasn't anything like I thought it would be. The place was kind of cool, and everyone who worked at the grief center was friendly.

We went back to the grief support center a week after the tour. First thing I noticed were the pizza boxes. Good start. I love pizza. I grabbed a slice. We were going to stay for an hour and a half, and for the first half hour, Mom, Debbie, and I sat at one of the round tables with some of the other parents and kids who had experienced all kinds of losses.

After we had finished eating our pizza, we moved to a huge fuzzy orange rug in the middle of the room. The adults and kids all sat in a circle. We passed around a talking stick. The person holding the stick was supposed to say his or her name and the name of the person who died. When I got the stick, I told them that my name was Alex and that my dad died.

On the walls of the room were paper drawings of elephants and a big tree. Pasted to the branches of the tree were paper leaves, stars, and snowflakes. Kids had written all kinds of things on them like, *I love you, Mom* or *I will miss you forever, Dad.*

The kids were grouped by age and taken to different rooms. Each room had chairs, bean bags, and over-sized cushions, and we could sit wherever we wanted. Mom was in a group with the other parents. Debbie's group was filled with the younger kids who had had all kinds of losses. It was good for her to be with kids her age. I'm her big brother and always make sure that Debbie's okay.

Debbie's room had an easel, a table with four chairs, a few bean bags on the floor, and a doll house. The bookcase had games like Twister and Operation, and a few dolls too. There was a clothesline, and pictures that kids had drawn were hanging on it. A puppet theater at the far end of the room had lots of room in back and a small stage in front. Debbie could create her own puppet show in there.

There were a lot of games and toys in each of the meeting rooms. There was a separate arts and crafts room with all kinds of stuff to do. There was a separate high-energy room where we could go when we needed to let off some steam. Our room even had a foosball table. I played with a boy named Sid whose little sister had died from cancer. She was only seven. That confused me. I couldn't even imagine something happening to my sister.

I won the coin flip and tossed the ball into play. We were kind of serious at first, but after shouting out "goal" several times, we started to loosen up. Sid didn't spin the soccer guys as quickly as some of my friends. While we played, he told me about his sister, and I told him about my dad. He scored five times and won. I had a good time, even though I was talking about my dad.

The kids in my group were around my age. Most of them were in the same grade as I was or maybe a year older than me. I talked to a girl, Autumn, whose dad had died of cancer. Autumn went to the grief center while her dad was on hospice. She said hospice helped her dad the year before he died. Autumn described a special room down the hall that looked like a room in a hospital with a large doll in the bed. The room reminded Autumn of her dad's room. Autumn said she was able to say goodbye to her dad there. While she was talking, all I could think about was how I wish I could have said goodbye to my dad, too.

I met another boy, Mike, whose dad had killed himself. We played Jenga in the corner of the room. It's a game with fifty-four blocks. I built the tower. We each took turns taking one block out of the tower. It gave us plenty of time to talk about our dads. Mike told me about his dad, and I told him about mine. He said he was sorry that my dad had died, and I knew he meant it. I told him how sorry I was that his father also had killed himself. I could tell that Mike was sad, just like me. But then he took a block out of the tower and the blocks fell all around the table and floor. We both laughed really hard while we were picking them up. Then we played Jenga one more time.

While Debbie and I were in our groups, Mom met with the other parents.

When I met up with Mom afterward, Debbie had been telling Mom about a picture that she had drawn. Mom looked at me and asked, "How did it go?"

"We played. We did art."

"And . . ."

"And they have lots of games like Battleship, Life, and Scrabble."

"That sounds like fun."

"We ate snacks. One of the kids had a brother who died. He was in the marines."

"How terribly sad."

"One kid said that his brother died because of drugs, and a girl said that her mom was murdered. I met Heidi. She said that her brother Scott was killed in a car accident with his cousin. They both died."

Gently, Mom asked, "Sounds to me like you heard a lot of stories. Are you okay?"

"Yeah, Mom. One of the boys said that his father had a heart attack. His uncle drove to school to pick him up and take him home to be with his mom."

"Wow. Just like you."

We started walking out of the center. "And Mom, I met a boy named Mike. His dad killed himself, too."

"I guess it helped you to see that you're not alone. Other kids are going through tough times, too."

"Mom, one of the girls, Alicia, showed me her mom's necklace. She likes wearing it. I told her about Dad's baseball cap."

"It looks like you have some things in common with these kids. Your dad's baseball cap is a special object for you. It links you to Dad because he always wore it."

"It reminds me of him, Mom."

"Every now and then a reminder can make us feel sad. But reminders also keep us connected to the people who we loved."

"I loved Dad."

"I know you did. Anything else you want me to know about your group?"

"There were all these different rooms that we were allowed to go into."

On the sidewalk outside the center, we stopped, and I handed my mom a picture that I had drawn. As I pointed to the picture, I explained, "Debbie and I are at the zoo. See, you are there, too. The three of us are eating bananas and staring at the monkeys in the cage."

"The monkeys are staring right back at us and pointing to our bananas," Mom added.

"Dad is floating above us."

Mom said, "I see that. You drew Dad holding his stomach."

"Yeah, that's because he is laughing so hard."

"I like your picture. I like that you have Dad watching over us."

"It's like you taught me, Mom. Dad will watch over me when I need him to, and when I don't want him to, he won't."

"Exactly. Ready to go home?"

"Yeah. But I want to go back to my group again. We're going to make masks next time."

"Masks. Sounds interesting."

"Yeah. We're going to make memory boxes, too, Mom."

"Wow. I'd like to see yours when it's done . . . All right, let's go home."

Ten Years Later

More than 47,000 people die each year by suicide. I still can't believe that my dad was one of them. I went to the grief center every other week for several months. I liked the kids and really got to know them. It was a tough time in our lives, but somehow our being together helped.

I've been mulling over some of the lessons I learned during those first few months. First, I discovered that I was not alone, that other kids had similar feelings to mine. I had a chance to talk about feelings that I had pushed way down inside of me. I got to hear how other kids dealt with their sadness and that helped me. We played games and created projects that helped me to get out my feelings of anger and fear.

I also learned about keeping a bond with Dad. I made a list of the good things I remembered about him. The other kids wrote their lists, too. We placed them on the wall around the room. As I read what the other kids had written, I realized we all have memories and sharing them was a good thing. I keep that list folded in my desk.

Another time, I wrote a letter to my dad. As I debated whether to show it to my mom, I heard my dad's voice in my head saying, "*You got the green light on that, Champ.*" That was what my dad always said whenever he gave me permission to do something. Those very words. I could still hear his voice. I wondered if I would ever forget what he sounded like. I gave myself the green light and shared the letter with my mom.

A few days ago, at a frat party, I noticed some guys were playing Jenga. In that moment I was transported back to the grief center where I had spoken to Mike, whose dad had killed himself. We had played Jenga in the corner of the room that day. I remember it so clearly—the sadness I felt at the same time having fun with Mike.

Every now and then, I still have those deep feelings of sadness. Other times, I just want to have fun. And I have learned that's okay.

Yesterday, I heard my dad's favorite song by Queen on the radio. I blasted the volume, and belted out the words, "We will rock you" at the top of my lungs—just like Dad used to do.

Follow-Up Questions

- In what ways can you relate to the family in Chapter 8?

- If you have attended a bereavement support group, what has it been like for you?

- If you have not attended a bereavement support group, would you like to go to one?

- Describe the part of your loss experience that you once thought you would never tell anyone about.

- Are you okay having fun or do you feel that you shouldn't be happy?

- If you could play a song on the radio for your loved one right now, what song would you choose?

- Alex's personality traits (e.g., team player, sensitive, sociable) helped him to talk about his dad's death with other bereaved children. How did you reveal your strengths to others at such a sad point in your life?

CHAPTER 9

Three Months Later

I've been wearing my dad's T-shirts and baseball cap a lot in the three months since he died. It feels good wearing things that belonged to him. Grandma has promised to give me Dad's watch when I am older. A few days ago, I let her read the letter that I had written to Dad after he died. We talked about it, and Grandma told me stories about my dad when he was a little boy.

Grandma gave me an album with photographs of my dad as a kid. I liked seeing him and my uncles as little boys on their bikes or splashing in the pool. Grandma told me I looked like my dad in one of the pictures. That's the one I took out of the album and keep on my desk. I like looking at my dad's photo. I have brought it with me both times that Mom, Debbie, and I went to the cemetery. I get anxious when I visit my dad's grave. It reminds me that my dad is really dead and that his body is in the ground. I just try to imagine him in heaven.

I am still going to the grief center every two weeks. The last time I went, we made a memory box. I decorated the box with some of Dad's buttons from his favorite shirts, and pictures I took at the zoo. I wrote "DAD" on the memory box and filled it with things that reminded me of him: his tie, a ticket stub, and a shiny pressed penny from Disney World.

When Mom saw the memory box, she wanted to do something together to celebrate my dad's life. So, Mom helped me to make a collage. We looked through magazines and cut out pictures that reminded us of Dad from those magazines. Then I glued them to a large piece of paper. I found pictures of a wooden desk, a coffee cup, and a donut. My dad loved donuts. Mom found a picture of a monkey and a fishing pole. I also found a picture of a baseball cap, a sports car, a TV, and Chinese food. They all became a part of the collage. Creating the collage made me feel close to my dad.

After we finished the collage, Mom and I watched a TV show about a time machine that transported the characters back in time. She asked me which day I would choose if I could go back in time to a day with Dad.

"I'd choose the day Dad died," I said. "I'd go back in time to that day."

"Why that day?"

"In order to change things. Mom, this time, I would miss the bus. I would make up a story."

"A story?" Mom asked.

"I would make up a story, so I wouldn't have to go to school."

"What would you say?"

"I would pretend that I didn't feel well. I would stay home and tell Dad how much I needed him."

"Tell him that you needed him . . . for what?"

"To help me study. I would ask him to help me practice for my assembly. I wouldn't leave him alone."

"Hmm, I see," Mom said. "Unfortunately, we can't go back in time, Alex."

"But if we could, Mom, I would have talked about baseball or my rock collection with Dad to keep his mind on something else. I would do everything I could to let him know that I loved him—that I needed him. I would not leave him alone for a minute."

"Alex, if you had stayed by his side all day, do you think that you could have prevented his death?" Mom asked.

"Yeah, Mom."

"No, sweetie. There was nothing you could have done."

I didn't believe her. "I could have saved him. I know it."

"Alex."

In my mind, it always came back to this—I should have saved my father. "It's my fault," I insisted. "I should have stayed home."

"Alex, you're blaming yourself for something you had no control over."

"I should have known he was going to kill himself."

"How? Could you read his mind? Did you know what he was thinking all the time?"

"Well, no—"

"Then why are you blaming yourself?" Mom asked.

"Because I didn't know he was going to do it—but I should have known."

"So, you feel guilty about not knowing."

"Mom, if I had known, I would have stopped him from killing himself. I made a mistake."

Mom looked me in the eye. "I get what you're saying. But it was your dad who made the mistake. Maybe when people want to end their lives, nothing will stop them."

I was angry at my mom and said loudly, "Mom, you could have stopped him. You were home."

Mom took a deep breath and shook her head. "I didn't know he was going to kill himself either. Dad was getting help from a therapist. I thought he was fine."

I screamed, "He wasn't fine, Mom!"

Mom started to cry, "You're right. Dad wasn't thinking clearly."

I wanted to punch something. I rammed my fist into a pillow on the sofa. "Why did he do this?"

"We are all trying to figure it out."

"Grandpa said Dad was depressed. Grandma said his brain chemicals weren't working right. Uncle Sammy said Dad couldn't cope. Everybody says something different."

"Alex, maybe we're all looking for answers. But only Dad knows the answer to the questions we are struggling with. Although we should talk about Dad's suicide, we need to focus on our feelings rather than try to find answers."

I punched the pillow again. "I should never have gotten onto that school bus."

"In reality you had no idea that Dad was going to end his life on that particular day. There was no reason for you to *not* get on the school bus."

"But I left him at home, and he killed himself."

"Think about that morning. What was on your mind? Were you thinking about going to school or about leaving your father so he could end his life?"

"Going to school."

"Exactly!"

"I wish I had a time machine. I know that I could have stopped him, and I didn't."

"It must be hard for you to feel this way."

"I let him down, Mom."

"How did you let him down?"

I started to shout. "Because I went to school instead of staying home. I left him alone. Don't you get it?"

"I get it. I know you're mad at yourself for not staying home." Mom took the pillow away from me and held my hand. "You're a child. Children go to school. That was your job on that morning."

"I didn't do the right thing. If I had been home, Dad wouldn't have killed himself," I insisted.

"Was that your job? Did someone tell you that you were supposed to stay home from school?"

"No . . ."

"Was I home with your dad?"

"Yeah, and you should have saved him," I yelled, as I began banging my fist on my knees.

Mom took a deep breath. "You're angry with me for not saving Dad."

I didn't want to hurt her any more than she was already hurting, but I was hurting, too. "Why didn't we know, Mom? Why didn't we do something?"

Tears slipped from my eyes.

Mom said, "We didn't have the chance."

Barely able to speak, I mumbled, "He made a huge mistake."

"It was the biggest mistake your dad could ever have made," Mom said. She put her arm around me, and we leaned into each other.

The next day, I visited my Uncle Sammy. I took the collage with me because I wanted to show it to him. Mom dropped me off in front of his house. The driveway was really icy, and I slipped several times, holding the collage over my head.

I finally reached the door of my uncle's house and let myself in. As I turned to wave to my mom, I saw that she was laughing at the sight of me struggling up the driveway. Mom used to laugh all the time. It felt good to see her laugh . . . sure, it was at my expense, but it still felt good.

My uncle was in the kitchen frying bacon. He always made bacon when my dad and I stopped by. But this time, my dad wasn't with me . . . even the smell of bacon reminded me of my dad. While my uncle and I ate one slice of bacon after another, he mentioned that he had not been back to visit Dad's grave at the cemetery. He said that he didn't want to look at any photos of my dad, either. My uncle had removed all of the photographs in which Dad appeared.

After we watched TV for a while, Uncle Sammy took me out for dinner. As I got into the truck, it felt weird sitting in the front seat next to him. I felt shaky, like I did three months ago, when he picked me up from school and told me my dad had died. At the restaurant, I told him that it was hard for me to sit in his truck. He said that he felt the same way because it brought back bad memories for him, too.

"Your mom gave me a book about grief to help me with my feelings," he said. "I've been reading it."

"Mom's been reading a lot of books about grief lately, too."

"The book helped me understand suicide a bit more."

Uncle Sammy explained how situations that remind him of Dad can make him feel angry or sad.

"Those things that cause me to react are called triggers. Your dad's death made me feel so helpless. I had never felt like that before. But even though something very sad and unexpected happened, having you around is calming."

"I like being with you, too, Uncle Sammy."

"Alex, certain triggers make me feel angry or shaky. Sometimes sitting in the truck is a trigger for me. What about you? Do you have any triggers?"

I understood what he was saying. I felt the same way. I told him about the first time I went into the basement after my dad died, and how I panicked and ran back up the stairs.

Uncle Sammy said, "That was a trigger. What were you afraid of?"

"It felt weird to see the place where Dad died."

"Would it help if your mom went with you the next time you go into the basement?"

"Maybe."

"In time, you'll probably be less afraid to go down there by yourself. I'm hoping that's the case with my truck. I can see how going to the place where your dad died could be upsetting. Ask your mom or me to go with you when you need to go into the basement, until you feel safe enough to go down there on your own."

"I'm not in any hurry, Uncle Sammy."

After talking about what I was afraid of, together we figured out that there was nothing there that could hurt me. It looked exactly as it had before my dad died. My uncle told me that whenever I go down to the basement, I should think about all the happy times my dad and I would play ping-pong there—or the times when he would teach me about the water heater, the furnace, and the fuse box. My dad made sure I knew about those things.

Ten Years Later

It took almost a year for Uncle Sammy to once again display the photos of him and dad around his house. And it took a couple of years for him to return to the diner where he and my dad had met every week. I guess it just takes some people longer than others to adjust to loss. Uncle Sammy had to learn how to live without his brother, just like I had to learn to live without my dad.

Every now and then, I think about the conversations Dad and I would have had if he had sat next to me as I drove us to Uncle Sammy's house for a plate of bacon. The car is my place to talk to Dad. It's where I tell him that he should have stayed around for me. Taught me how to shave. Been at my high school graduation. And next year, I'll probably tell him that he should have been sitting next to Mom when I graduate from college.

I drove home this weekend to visit my mom. While Debbie was blow-drying her hair, Mom and I talked about the memory box I had made years ago. Mom was standing at the kitchen counter, using the blender to make strawberry shakes. I flashed to a memory of Dad reminding Mom to not use the blender when anyone was using the blow-dryer. It always blew a fuse.

As if right on cue, the room went dark. Although I knew what to do, a big part of me wanted to stay far away from the basement. That's where my dad had died. It felt strange walking down the steps to flip the switch. I thought about how Dad had walked those same steps to end his life. Here I am, a grown man, feeling like a child. I guess it's because I am his child and still miss him very much.

A part of me wanted to hang out in the basement. Another part of me wanted to stay far away from the place where my dad had died. My mom told me that it was normal to be scared, nervous, or frustrated. I have figured out ways to distract myself when a trigger tries to get the best of me. Every now and then, I think about the rocks and fossils my dad and I collected. I know it may sound strange, but thinking about rocks actually helps me feel better.

When it was safe to resume using the blender, my mom finished making the shakes. We talked about school, and then we talked about my dad. I told her that I still talk to him and ask him questions like: Why didn't you come to me? Or why did God allow this to happen? While sipping our shakes, we watched a television show in which one of the characters kills himself. It took both of us by surprise. People in the show were being judgmental, talking about how suicide was a selfish act. I wanted to scream at the screen. My dad was not selfish. He was in emotional pain and was not thinking clearly. My dad would never have intentionally hurt anyone, especially me. By the time my mom asked me if we could change the channel, I was one step ahead of her. I had already picked up the remote to do just that.

Follow-Up Questions

- In what ways can you relate to the family in Chapter 9?

- How long has it been since your loved one died?

- Do you wear something that belonged to your loved one?

- What do you consider the best reason for keeping a special object that belonged to the deceased?

- Have people confused you by giving you different explanations for why someone dies by suicide?

- What questions do you still have about what happened?

- If you could go back in time to be with the person who died, which day would you choose?

- What made you choose this particular day?

- When you experience a trigger, what thoughts help you feel better?

- Is there something that you have avoided doing because it reminds you of the person who died?

- Alex's personality traits (e.g., creative, imaginative, respectful) helped him cope in the months after his dad died. How did using your strengths in the few months after your loss help you to manage what you were going through?

CHAPTER 10

One Year Anniversary

I stood at my dad's grave with my mom, Debbie, Uncle Sammy, Aunt Jillian, Uncle Alan, Grandma, and Grandpa. It was the one-year anniversary of Dad's death.

"I miss you so much," Mom said, as she held Debbie's hand and looked down at the grave.

Grandpa said, "No father should ever have to bury his son. I love you, Bill."

Touching the headstone, Grandma said, "Bill, I still pick up the phone to call you, thinking that you're at work."

"Football games just aren't the same, bro," said Uncle Sammy, staring at Dad's gravestone.

I had a lot to say but no words with which to say them; I remained silent with my head bowed.

That day everyone would be coming back to the house to gather and give each other support. That was part of the job of anniversaries —making sure we are not alone. Mom had made tons of food, all of my dad's favorites. As we walked to the car, she said, "My friend Chris is coming over too. She made Dad's favorite cookies."

"Oh, Mom, Chris puts a million chocolate chips in her cookies."

"I know she does. That's why Dad loved them."

"I can't wait to eat those cookies," Debbie said.

When we got to the house, Grandma assigned everyone a job. Grandpa and I folded the napkins. Aunt Jillian made iced tea, while Mom made two pots of coffee. Chris and Uncle Sammy set the table.

Uncle Alan put a large dish of spaghetti and meatballs in the middle of the table. Dad always said that Mom made the "best meatballs on the planet."

As she stirred the pitcher of iced tea, Aunt Jillian started talking to my mom about growth and how resilient people can experience personal growth when something terrible happens to them. But those with less resilience can experience posttraumatic growth.

Mom asked, "Posttraumatic growth?"

"Sherry, it's when a person who is less resilient changes in a positive way and grows from a traumatic loss," my aunt explained. "Hey, Alex, I bet you have strengths you probably didn't even know you had before your dad died."

"Yeah, I'm pretty strong, Aunt Jillian."

"When I think about your strengths, I think how you are brave and thoughtful."

"Thanks, Aunt Jillian."

"Although I have put my strengths into practice, I see myself differently now. Suicide awareness is important to me. It's a positive that came out of all this. What about you, Alex, any positive changes?" Aunt Jillian asked.

"Positive? Hmmm . . . I'm thankful for my mom. I didn't appreciate her before my dad died as much as I do now."

Mom gave me a smile. "Oh, thank you for saying that. I'm so thankful for you, too."

"And I'm grateful for everyone in this family," Grandma said.

"You know, I'm also grateful to the folks in my suicide loss support group," said Mom. "They're not judgmental. They accept me. I've seen lots of growth in that group. What do you think about all this, Dad?"

"Sherry, I don't know if I have grown from this experience at all.

I lost my son. He was a good boy. Life is short. That's all I've got to say," Grandpa said.

Uncle Alan said, "We're lucky that we have each other. Some people have a friend or a neighbor that helps them get through times like this. We all get by in our own way."

"You know what worked for me this year?" Mom said. "I learned about deep breathing, muscle relaxation, and guided imagery. I've started practicing yoga."

"You found ways to cope, Sherry. You really are resilient," Aunt Jillian said.

"Sherry is my most resilient friend," Chris said, placing a plate of cookies on the table.

"All of us are resilient. I realize that now," Mom said. "Bill, on the other hand, was not resilient. He had a suicide plan. He took the day off, which he never did. He made sure the kids were not at home. He had the means to get help, but . . . I wish he had been as resilient as the rest of us."

I felt the big question in the room, the one that never goes away: Why did he do it?

While Grandma and Mom kept giving everyone tasks to do, Aunt Jillian said, "From what I'm learning, people die of suicide because of a mix of their environment, biology, and history."

"I read about that, too: they're called risk factors. But I still don't know why Bill killed himself," Mom said.

"Maybe it had something to do with his physical or mental health," Aunt Jillian said. "If he had distorted thinking and access to a way to kill himself, well, maybe that's the answer to the question of 'why.'"

"Lots of people are stressed out and have access to a means, but they don't kill themselves. Come on, Jillian, I don't think that's the reason Bill ended his life," Uncle Sammy stated.

"Maybe it's because of genetics," Aunt Jillian said.

Uncle Alan shook his head. "I don't know of anyone else in the family who has killed himself."

"People at risk can attempt suicide more than once," Chris said. "Another risk factor is having an abusive childhood."

"Come on, Chris. Bill had a great childhood. We're not even getting warmer," Grandpa said.

"And Bill never attempted suicide before," Uncle Alan said. He shook his head. "Here we are trying to figure out why Bill killed himself while all I do is reconstruct what he did over and over again in my head. I agonize about his being in that much psychological pain."

"I've read a lot about suicide awareness, but I just don't know. Maybe he killed himself because of a brain disease or because of certain personality traits," Jillian added.

"I know that he didn't have any job or financial problems," Grandma said.

I didn't understand everything about risk factors. I just knew that sometimes when I thought about Dad, I felt frustrated. Finally, I said, "Maybe we will never know why."

Everyone in the room paused for a moment and looked at me. Uncle Sammy said, "It might take us a long time to figure out why Bill killed himself."

"Or, like Alex says, we may never know," Uncle Alan said.

"Still, it's okay to keep asking the question, whether or not we ever figure out the answer," Uncle Sammy said.

Mom sighed. "Well, in any case, it's been a rough year."

"It has been," Aunt Jillian agreed, "but it would have been a lot rougher without resilience. That's what has helped me recover emotionally from all of this. I had to do something. So, I chose to focus on suicide awareness."

Mom said, "What works for me is keeping Bill's memory alive for my kids and letting them know it's okay to share their feelings."

"It's good that we talk about Bill, and how we're coping. I really can't believe that a whole year has passed," Uncle Sammy said.

Mom announced that the food—all of Dad's favorites—was ready. As I sat down next to Debbie, I noticed that there was an empty chair where Dad used to sit. Mom told me beforehand that she was going to leave one extra chair at the table for Dad.

No one said anything about the chair as they ate their food. So, I decided to say something. "I know that Dad would have loved all this food. He may not be here eating it with us, but I know he's watching and he's glad that we're together."

Mom said, "Bill would have loved all of this food."

I looked at Mom and said, "Best meatballs on the planet."

Mom smiled, remembering that Dad would always say that whenever he ate the meatballs and spaghetti she made.

Holding up his glass of iced tea, Uncle Sammy said, "To Bill, we love you and will always remember you."

Everyone lifted their glasses. We ate . . . we talked . . . we laughed . . . and we remembered Dad.

Ten Years Later

Suicide is the tenth leading cause of death in the U.S., and today is the ten-year anniversary of my dad's death. I drove home from college to be with my mom. She invited her friend Chris, my grandparents, and my aunt and uncles to go to the cemetery. Just as she had done on the day that all of us had gathered at the graveside on the one-year anniversary, Mom held Debbie's hand the whole time. Mom cried really hard; I thought she would never stop. When Mom finally did stop crying, we went home and had a big dinner. It wasn't Thanksgiving, but it felt like it with all my dad's favorite foods. Mom, the maker of the best meatballs on the planet, made spaghetti and meatballs, of course.

While we ate, my mom recalled what it was like for her right after my dad died. "Those first days were such a blur," Mom said. Because I was young at that time, I hadn't realized all the things that go into funeral planning: religious and cultural preferences at the grave site, military involvement, having a closed casket, selecting someone to give the eulogy, preparing newspaper notices, and choosing a cemetery, just to name a few of the details Mom had to take care of while she was falling apart. My dad's death broke my mom's heart and changed my world.

After dinner, Chris gave Mom a necklace with a pendant in the shape of a heart. My dad's face was etched on the heart. When I saw his face, I missed him even more. My mom vowed she would never take off the pendant.

Hearing Mom recollect her experience stirred up memories of my first year after Dad died. It went fast. My grief kept changing almost every day, from shock to confusion to anger and back again. At times I cried, and occasionally, I screamed. As the months passed, I still felt sad. I missed my dad a lot. I also felt angry that he had let me down. I was just a kid and needed him.

That first year, my feelings were like a yo-yo, swinging back and forth. At times I was angry and raw. Other times, I hung out with my friends, watched TV, played sports, or listened to music. I didn't feel sad or angry every single day. It was like a giant wave. Now and then, I struggled to keep my head above water; other times, I just wanted to ride the wave.

Right after Dad died, I was afraid I might forget all the good times that we had. Debbie had trouble remembering him. I was scared that I would forget him, too, but that never happened. I have accepted that my dad is dead and have forgiven him for ending his life. I'm thankful for my family and for still feeling my dad's presence with me every single day.

I learned a lot about grief that first year. I had to adjust and learn new skills in dealing with the tough times, especially the "firsts." Dad wasn't at my twelfth birthday party; he didn't pretend to blow out the candles on my cake as he'd always done. He wasn't there at Thanksgiving; he didn't cut the turkey, which was always his job. He didn't go on vacation with us. And he won't be there when I visit Aunt Jillian and Uncle Alan in Las Vegas to celebrate my twenty-first birthday.

Mom helped me keep the good memories alive and to find meaning in Dad's death. She helped me focus on my strengths and learn to forgive him. The relationships I have with my mom and with others in my family have become even more important to me since Dad died. I've definitely grown from this experience.

I have accepted the reality that my dad is dead. Although I tried to deny it at first, I know he is never coming home. Putting my dad's photograph on my desk helped me to accept that I will never see him again. It made me aware that even though I no longer have a dad who is alive, I have lots of good memories. I've dealt with my painful feelings. My world has changed.

I've learned a lot about suicide over the years and the stigma attached to it. Everyone in our family has. Mom learned some coping techniques from her therapist and taught them to me. Aunt Jillian turned her grief into action. She has helped a lot of people because she doesn't want anyone else to go through what we went through. She learned about a gatekeeper program. It's called Question, Persuade, Refer (QPR). It taught her how to recognize a person who is at risk for suicide. Aunt Jillian knows how to react and refer them for treatment. It's her way of finding meaning in my dad's death.

I'm always reminded of my dad at some point in the day. My mom has a lot of grief triggers. Mom wrote them all down: holidays, his birthday, waking up alone, the date he died, the smell of his cologne, hearing their favorite song on the radio, watching television, eating meals without him, and getting into bed to go to sleep and his not being there.

I thought about making my own list but changed my mind. I gave myself "the green light," as Dad would say, to manage my grief in my own way, share my story with those with whom I'm comfortable with, and to continue the bond with him for the rest of my life.

- In what ways can you relate to the family in Chapter 10?
- What do you do now to distract yourself from grief?
- Do you have a special place where you keep reminders of your loved one?
- What do you value most about what your loved one taught you?
- Are you doing anything now that would make the person who died proud of you?
- Of all the "firsts," which ones were especially hard for you?
- What do you feel are the best ways to handle "the firsts"?
- What good times with your loved one do you remember?
- List three things for which you are thankful.
- What are some of the biggest changes in your life since the death of your loved one?
- Have you experienced any personal growth or post-traumatic growth because of your loss?
- What part of your story are you least likely to share with others?
- What is different about your grief today, as compared to one year ago?
- In what specific ways would you like to honor your loved one?
- Alex's personality traits (e.g., forgiving, spiritual, reflective) helped him cope a year after the death of his dad. In what ways did you put your strengths into action several months or years after the death of your loved one?

Appendix

APPENDIX A

PALETTE OF GRIEF®

What is a Palette of Grief?

Palette of Grief is an activity that visually captures grief reactions. Metaphors are the use of rhetorical expression that helps you fully grasp your narrative, which is your story of loss. What would your grief look like if you describe it as an image or object? You may describe what happened as a journey or a roller coaster ride.

For the metaphor, Palette of Grief, the primary concept is an artist's palette, which is a thin and usually oval flat tablet with a thumbhole at one end that painters hold and use to blend paint colors. When the palette is metaphorically applied to loss, it becomes that which holds and blends physical, emotional, cognitive, behavioral, and spiritual reactions after a final separation.

Where Did the Idea of Palette of Grief Come From?

Barbara Rubel, a suicide loss survivor, found that watercolor painting helped her understand her grief process after her father's suicide. One day, almost finished with a painting, Barbara spilled a glass of water on her palette, which caused the colors to mix into one another. This made her think how grief reactions often blend together.

Brief Description

The task is to create an image of a palette that captures your overall reactions to loss. The graphic image creatively spurs you to a deeper understanding of your grief reactions.

Suggestions for Use

This activity may be completed during support groups, individual counseling sessions, grief therapy, at home, and in healthcare and mental health professional training sessions. Although you may have experienced more than one loss, only focus on one loss per palette.

The Palette of Grief page can be copied before you begin the activity so you can create another palette for another loss. This activity can be used as a springboard to talk about your loss and, ultimately, find meaning in it.

Contraindications for Use

This activity is best suited for use after several weeks have passed since the loss. It should not be done if you are feeling acute intense reactions.

Materials and Supplies

1. Palette of Grief Activity

2. Five different color markers. In a group setting, there needs to be enough color markers so everyone will have the opportunity to use five different colors.

3. Tables are needed in order to write. If no tables are available, clipboards need to be distributed.

4. Optional classical music or meditation music can be played in the background.

Time Requirement

Minimum: 45 minutes. Maximum: 1½ hours.

Basic Procedure

There are five check boxes that refer to emotional, cognitive, behavioral, physical, and spiritual reactions on page 188. You will check off each of the boxes, one at a time, as you do the activity and then write your grief reactions within the artist's palette on page 189.

Instructions

Read *Let's Get Started* for an understanding of the context and an explanation of each of the five steps in this activity.

How to Interpret Your Palette of Grief

Once you have finished the activity, use "How to Interpret Your Palette" to understand your Palette of Grief.

Customizing the Procedure

In a group setting, individuals can share their palette with the persons sitting near them. You may also want to consider giving one or two individuals an opportunity to share how they have interpreted their palette with the entire group.

Follow-Up

At the completion of this activity, you can explore the Palette of Grief Guided Imagery.

Long-Term Follow-Up

Also, the activity can be repeated months after the initial creation of a Palette of Grief (e.g., three, six, and twelve months). Retain it for reference and comparison of reactions.

Comments

While the palette is being completed, a clinician, or group facilitator needs to ensure that everyone gets a chance to complete the activity and that time limits are respected.

Let's Get Started

Step 1—Emotional Reactions (Time frame: 5-10 minutes)
First, choose one color marker. Use this color ONLY for emotional reactions. Mark the emotional reaction box with a check mark on page 188. Review the page: Emotional Reactions. If you felt any of the emotions listed due to your loss, write the word(s) inside your palette on page 189. Write one word or several words. Write them large or small. Be as creative as you like.

Step 2—Cognitive Reactions (Time frame: 5-10 minutes)
Next pick a different marker to represent thoughts. Use this color ONLY for cognitive reactions. Mark the behavioral reactions box with a check mark on page 188. Review the page: Cognitive Reactions. If you thought about any of the words listed due to your loss, write the word(s) inside your palette on page 189.

Step 3—Behavioral Reactions (Time frame: 5-10 minutes)
Next, select a different marker to represent behaviors. Use this color ONLY for behavioral reactions. Mark the behavioral reactions box with a check mark on page 188. Review the page: Behavioral Reactions. If you conducted yourself in a certain way because of your loss, write the word(s) inside your palette on page 189.

Step 4—Physical Reactions (Time frame: 5-10 minutes)
Now choose a different marker to represent physical reactions. Use this color ONLY for physical reactions. Mark the physical reactions box with a check mark on page 188. Review the page: Physical Reactions. If you experienced any physical reactions because of your loss, write the word(s) inside your palette on page 189.

Step 5—Spiritual Reactions (Time frame: 5-10 minutes)

Finally, pick a different marker to represent spiritual reactions. Use this color ONLY for spiritual reactions. Mark the spiritual reactions box with a check mark on page 188. Review the page: Spiritual Reactions. If you experienced any spiritual reactions because of your loss, write the word(s) inside your palette on page 189.

You have completed the five steps. Although the Palette of Grief activity is enlightening, it can be exhausting. If overwhelmed, stop the activity. Focus on your breathing and relax.

Go to "How to Interpret Your Palette" when you feel ready to explore your grief process.

A Note to the Clinician

Imagine meeting a new bereaved client and being able to quickly attune to their grief process and actually see their emotional, cognitive, physical, behavioral, and spiritual reactions. Your sessions can now be extremely effective because you have a tool that visually captures your client's grief reactions. Use the "How to Interpret Your Palette" as a starting point to treat their grief symptoms when they have maladaptive thoughts or have a failure in emotional regulation. Remember that grief is not a mental illness to be treated. Rather, it is a normal process that at times, when it gets complicated, requires professional assistance.

Emotional Reactions

I am afraid of living.

I feel agitated.

I am aggravated.

I am angry.

I am anxious.

I am apathetic.

I am apprehensive.

I feel betrayed.

I am bewildered.

I am bitter.

I blame myself or someone else for the death.

I am bored.

I feel contempt.

I am in denial.

I feel despair.

I feel detached from others.

I am disgusted.

I am emancipated.

I miss being emotionally dependent.

I feel empty.

I am envious.

I have become estranged from my family.

I fear I might harm myself or others.

I am fearful of losing others.

I feel frazzled.

I am frustrated.

I am grateful.

I feel grouchy.

I feel guilty.

I feel helpless.

I am hurt.

I feel incomplete.

I feel jealous.

I am joyful.

I feel lonely.

I feel longing.

I feel lost.

I need to wear a mask to not show my real feelings.

I am moody.

I am emotionally numb.

I feel nervous.

I am outraged.

I am overwhelmed.

I feel panicky.

I am peaceful.

I am pessimistic.

I am puzzled.

I feel relief.

I feel rejected.

I feel sadness.

I have self-doubt.

I feel shame.

My world is shattered.

I feel emotionally shocked.

I have shut down.

I feel stigmatized.

I am surprised.

I am torn.

I feel useless.

I am vengeful.

I am worried.

I yearn for my loved one.

Cognitive Reactions

I have trouble accepting the death.

I am apathetic.

I avoid certain thoughts.

I avoid reminders.

I have a negative attitude.

I feel abandoned.

I am absentminded.

I don't belong.

I have brain fog.

I think I am going crazy.

I just can't believe it.

I am closed-minded.

I have trouble concentrating.

I feel contempt.

I am not in control.

I am confused.

I criticize myself.

I have trouble making decisions or plans.

I am disorientated.

I have exaggerated thinking.

I think I am a failure.

I have flashbacks.

I am flooded by my thoughts.

I am forgetful.

I have fragmented memories.

I have experienced hallucinations.

I deserve to be happy.

I have homicidal ideation.

I am hypervigilant.

I am indecisive.

I jump to conclusions.

I cannot let it out.

I think life is too hard to endure.

People are tired of listening to me.

I have learned negative things about my loved one that have changed my view of her/him.

My life just seems different.

I feel lost.

I fear I am losing my mind.

I have nightmares.

I obsess about things.

I'm oddly aware of things related to death.

I often think about how short life is.

I am outraged.

I am preoccupied with the deceased and/or with the circumstances of the death.

I must be perfect.

The perception I have of myself has changed.

I can't make sense out of it.

I have made sense out of it.

I have low self-esteem.

I don't feel safe.

I speculate on what should have been done for my loved one.

I did the best I could.

I think about taking my own life.

I think of my loved one all the time.

I have all-or-nothing thinking.

I have difficulty trusting others.

I have a sense of unreality.

I have unwanted pictures in my head.

I feel worthless.

I repeatedly ask, "Why?"

Behavioral Reactions

I put my feelings into my artwork.

I try to stay active.

I have decreased activities.

I am becoming aggressive.

I avoid reminders of the deceased.

I stay in bed all day.

I have kept the belongings of my loved one intact.

I bite my nails.

I call out to my deceased loved one.

I carry special objects.

I cry and feel tearful.

I have been careless and clumsy.

I have conflicts with coworkers.

My drug use is causing problems.

I have been drinking alcohol.

I am eating very little/too much.

I have become fidgety.

I seek forgiveness.

I have provided forgiveness.

I am compulsively gambling on the internet.

I have become introverted.

I have become impatient.

I am isolating myself from my usual networks.

I lose things.

I mistrust others.

I depend on caffeine and/or nicotine to regulate my mood and energy.

I am moody.

I listen to music now more than ever before.

I visit online bereavement message boards/chat rooms.

I organize to excessiveness.

I have outbursts.

I have become overprotective.

I pace.

I look at photos.

I procrastinate.

I am preoccupied.

I have become quiet.

I neglect my responsibilities.

I feel reckless.

I have difficulty with relationships.

I have restless hyperactivity.

I have changed my routine.

I seek out places.

I have problems with sexual functioning.

I have become self-destructive.

I find myself sighing a lot.

I am spending too much money.

I have sleep disturbances.

I am searching for clues.

I am having speech problems.

I need to facilitate a support group.

I have a strained face.

I grind my teeth.

I talk excessively.

I can't talk about it.

I talk about my loss in a grief support group.

I treasure certain items.

I work out at the gym more than ever before.

My work performance has changed.

Physical Reactions

I have aches/pains.

I have new food allergies.

I have arthritis.

I have asthma.

I have backaches.

I have difficulty catching my breath.

I have high blood pressure.

I have butterflies in my stomach.

I feel like I am carrying around a ton of bricks.

I have elevated cholesterol.

I have cardiovascular disease.

I have pounding heart, chest pain, or heartburn.

I have cold chills or hot flashes.

I have a lump in my throat.

I have frequent colds/decreased resistance to illness.

I am constipated.

I am depressed.

I have diarrhea.

I have dry mouth.

I feel dizzy.

I have worsening eczema.

I have lost my energy.

I am exhausted.

I have eye strain.

I have been feeling faint.

I am fatigued.

I grind my teeth.

I have headaches.

I have a rapid heartbeat.

I have increased hair loss.

I have hives.

I have insomnia.

I have "jelly legs."

I am lightheaded.

I feel muscle tension.

I am nauseous.

I have a pain in my neck.

I have a peptic ulcer.

I feel restlessness even though I am sitting still.

I feel run-down.

I feel intense pangs of separation distress.

My sexual desire has changed.

I feel shaky on the inside.

I find myself sighing a lot.

I have skin problems.

I have shortness of breath.

My sleep patterns have changed.

I have slowed down.

I'm easily startled by noise/touch.

I have stomach bloating or pain.

I have burning in the pit of my stomach.

I have trouble swallowing.

I suddenly sweat.

I have the same symptoms as the deceased.

I have nervous twitches.

I am very tense.

I am thirsty.

I tremble.

I frequently need to urinate.

I have an unsteady voice.

I feel weakened.

I experienced changes in weight.

I feel a void.

Spiritual Reactions

I have abandoned my faith.

I am apathetic about the future.

I make mental affirmations.

I believe in an afterlife.

I created an altar.

I believe in angels.

I feel awakened by my experience.

I have experiences of awe.

I have revised my beliefs.

My beliefs are a source of strength.

I feel blessed.

I have profound coincidences.

I continue the bonds with the deceased.

I have become cynical.

I have detected my loved one's cologne/perfume.

My loved one comes to me in dreams.

I search other faiths.

I need God's love more than ever.

I question why God let this happen.

I can no longer praise God.

I am angry at God.

I feel God's grace.

My view of God has changed.

I don't understand why God did not heal my loved one.

I don't think God cares about me.

My loss is a valuable lesson from God.

I believe that a loving God would never have let this happen.

My loved one is in heaven.

My loved one is in hell.

I heard the voice of the deceased.

I have felt my loved one's presence.

I saw the deceased for a moment.

I feel enlightened.

I have a stronger faith.

I feel forsaken.

I have offered my forgiveness.

I feel grateful.

I use my experience to help others.

I feel hopeless.

I feel hopeful.

I feel an inner peace.

I am joyful.

I feel judged.

I judge others.

I believe in karma.

My life is meaningless.

I have a greater love for things.

I found meaning in what happened.

I question the meaning of my life.

I meditate.

I no longer believe in miracles.

I have difficulty moving on.

I have noticed objects move or disappear/reappear.

I search for proof of life after death.

I find comfort through prayer.

My sense of purpose has changed.

I create rituals that help me.

I no longer attend religious services.

I question why people suffer.

I attend services more than ever.

I enjoy singing hymns.

I have difficulty attending a place of worship.

I believe the world is a bad place.

Check the Box

As you work through the 5 steps, use this page and pages 190-191 to interpret your palette.

☐ **Emotional Reactions**

☐ **Cognitive Reactions**

☐ **Behavioral Reactions**

☐ **Physical Reactions**

☐ **Spiritual Reactions**

How to Interpret Your Palette

Refer to the five checked boxes as a reminder of what each color represents. Palette of Grief will become the starting point that helps you manage your grief reactions. Here are questions to consider:

• Are you surprised by the way your palette turned out?

• What beliefs do you have about yourself now that you finished a Palette of Grief?

• What value do you get out of seeing your reactions on a Palette of Grief?

• Has your Palette of Grief given you a greater perspective about loss?

• If a color stands out, what type of reaction does it represent?

• Which three words on your palette are you comfortable discussing?

• If there is a word that is upsetting, what is the significance of that word?

• Did you deliberately exclude some words because it was too painful to write them down?

• Do you believe that your grief reactions should be avoided?

• Do you believe that your grief reactions should be accepted?

• Have you given yourself permission to grieve?

• Do you believe that if you shared your palette with others who are bereaved, it would help you feel connected to them?

• Can you predict what will happen if you find positive ways to manage your grief?

How to Interpret Your Palette

- Can any positive psychological change occur due to your struggling with your grief reactions?

- Have you been through any other experiences recently that is making your grief more difficult to deal with?

- Do you find it painful to self-reflect?

- In what ways do you distract yourself from your grief?

- In what way has your grief process changed the way you look at your world?

- Is your grief process compromising your health?

- Are there any grief reactions that are draining your energy?

- What coping skills and inner strengths are you using to manage your grief?

- With a sense of curiosity, what do you want to explore now that you have finished your Palette of Grief?

- Can you make meaning out of your Palette of Grief?

APPENDIX B

PALETTE OF GRIEF®
GUIDED IMAGERY FOR SUICIDE LOSS SURVIVORS

The Palette of Grief can be experienced to a clinically significant level. This visualization is a guided imagery script in which you imagine walking along a path. Three parts of this script may be uncomfortable. Take a break and respect your limits. Stop at any point.

Customize the Procedure

There are three ways to use this guided imagery.

- Slowly read the guided imagery to yourself. Pause often to experience the relaxing nature of the script.

- Ask another person to recite the guided imagery to you. Make sure that the person speaks slowly and pauses often.

- Tape yourself or someone else slowly reading the script and then listen to the recording.

Room Setup

This is a seated guided visualization. Find a comfortable place to sit and remain seated throughout the visualization. Keep distractions to a minimum.

Time Requirement

Thirty minutes. The guided imagery is designed to be read or listened to in an unhurried manner. The pace is slow to allow you time to focus on the experience.

Visualization Script

Picture yourself in a relaxing place. Sit comfortably as you bring your awareness to your body. Be patient with yourself as you sit in the stillness. Move around a bit to get loosened up. Notice any unpleasant sensations. Sit up straight. Then let all your muscles go loose and feel your body relax.

Slowly breathe through your nose. Feel your nostrils fill with air. Exhale through your mouth. Breathe through your nose again. Exhale through your mouth. Notice the rhythm of your breath. Pace your breath, as you do this guided imagery.

Guide your attention to your neck. Tense your neck muscles. Slowly release the tension. Bring your attention to your head. Gently roll your head in a small circle, then reverse. Allow your face to be calm. Sigh deeply. Let the air leave your lungs. Slowly breathe through your nose and exhale through your mouth.

Guide your attention to your back. Slowly move around to alleviate any tension in your back. Bring your awareness to your shoulder blades. Gradually extend your spine to the sky. Roll your shoulder blades. Drop your shoulders back down. Feel the tension release.

Bring your awareness to your upper arms. Be still as you move down to your lower arms. Guide your awareness to your wrists, palms, and fingertips. Slowly sense the energy in your fingertips.

Bring awareness to your hands. Stretch out your fingers and slowly make a fist three times. Then let your hands gently fall on your thighs.

Now, put your arms in front of you like you are pressing a ball into water. Do this a few times. Move at your own pace. Then let your hands gently fall on your thighs.

Now that you have loosened up, think about a peaceful place that you have already been to or one you would like to visit and picture yourself taking a walk. Bring your awareness to a long inviting path in front of you. Continue to breathe slowly.

Approach and become aware of your surroundings. It feels safe. Listen to the soothing sounds. What are you curious about as you envision this healing place?

Visualize yourself moving ahead. As you walk, your feet feel light beneath you. Pay attention to your legs. Imagine your legs lighter than air, lifting you into each step. Take your time.

As you look ahead, you notice a person sitting on a large rock. You have yearned to see this person again. Sit on the rock. Observe how your body feels as it contacts the rock. This person wants to listen to you and help you to let go of sorrow or emptiness you might be feeling. Notice the thoughts that are occurring with this experience. Stay here for a few moments and tell this person what you need to say.

What does speaking to this person mean to you? Is there any benefit in speaking with this person? (Pause.)

It is time to say goodbye to this person. Focus on how you are feeling as you say goodbye. Take a healing breath. Inhale through your nose and exhale through your mouth. Exhale anything that doesn't comfort you. You feel grounded. Do this at your own pace.

Continue on the path. Notice how your legs feel. The ground is firm. Become aware of the landscape. Look up to the open sky. The path is winding. The walk feels good.

As you look ahead, you notice someone sitting on a wooden bench. As you approach, you recognize this person. As you slowly walk toward the bench, your feet feel lighter than air. Be mindful of what you are sensing as you walk toward this person. Your eyes meet and you sit down. This person needs to tell you something. Listen to the words being said. What does their voice sound like? Listen to what you need to hear. (Pause.)

Reflect on the lasting words this person has spoken to you. Use your imagination. Let this person know how their words make you feel. Say goodbye when you are ready. (Pause.)

What does listening to this person mean to you? Is there any benefit in listening to this person? (Pause.)

Now, imagine yourself walking along a path. Picture yourself in a peaceful, safe place. Stop for a moment and notice your surroundings. See the colors around you. What do you see? What sounds do you hear? What do you smell? Allow this place to nourish you. (Pause.)

You notice a rectangular wooden chest in front of you. The sunlight is shining on the chest. Open the hinged dome lid and look inside. A letter is leaning against the cloth upholstery. Take the time to read the letter that is addressed to you. When you are done reading, place it back inside the chest or do with it as you wish. (Pause.)

Who wrote you the letter? What does this person need to tell you? (Pause.)

Has the letter helped you with any confusion you might be feeling? Can you identify what you are feeling in this moment? (Pause.)

What does reading the letter mean to you? Is there any benefit found in reading this letter? (Pause.)

The time has come to take a path that leads you home. Allow peace and light to pass through your body. Scan your body for any place that still feels tense. Pay attention to the sensation and let go of the tension. Recognize the tiny changes that are happening in your body. (Pause.)

Take a healing breath. Witness the breath as it enters your body. Witness it again as you exhale.

Take a healing breath. Inhale through your nose and exhale through your mouth.

Take a healing breath. As you bring your attention back to the outer world, slowly stretch out your arms in front of you to the point of mild tension. Slowly bring your shoulders forward, up, and back. Do these shoulder curls two times.

Slowly push your right palm toward the ceiling, while pushing your left palm toward the floor. Then slowly push your left palm toward the ceiling, while pushing your right palm toward the floor.

Next, place your hands on your heart. Be aware of how you are feeling as the exercise ends.

References

American Psychiatric Association. (2013). *Diagnostic and statistical manual of mental disorders* (5th ed.). Washington, DC: Author.

American Psychiatric Association (n.d.). *Helping residents cope with a patient's suicide.* https://www.psychiatry.org/residents-medical-students/residents/coping-with-patient-suicide

Andriessen, K. (2009). Can postvention be prevention? *Crisis, 30*(1), 43-47. http://doi.org/10.1027/0227-5910.30.1.43

Andriessen, K., Mowll, J., Lobb, E., Draper, B., Dudley, M., & Mitchell, P. B. (2018). "Don't bother about me." The grief and mental health of bereaved adolescents. *Death Studies, 0*(0), 1-24. https://doi.org/10.1080/07481187.2017.1415393

Armour, M. (n.d.). *Aftermath of violent death.* http://www.survivorresources.org/grief-knowledge/articles-survivors/aftermath-of-violent-death/

Association for Death Education and Counseling. (2015). *Body of knowledge matrix.* https://www.adec.org/adec/Main/Continuing_Education/Body_of_Knowledge_Matrix/ADEC_Main/Earn-Certification/Body_of_Knowledge_M.aspx?hkey=6e6b4ce8-3e91-4578-a5dc-d614050160db

Attig, T. (2001). Relearning the world: Making and finding meanings. In R. Neimeyer (Ed.), *Meaning reconstruction and the experience of loss* (pp. 33-54). Washington, DC: American Psychological Association.

Bartel, B. T. (2019). Families grieving together: Integrating the loss of a child through ongoing relational connections. *Death Studies,* 1-12. doi:10.1080/07481187.2019.1586794

Beyers, J. M., Rallison, L., & West, C. (2017). Dialogical space in grief work: Integrating the alterity of loss. *Death Studies, 41*(7), 427-435. https://doi.org/10.1080/07481187.2017.1288666

Blackburn, P., & Bulsara, C. (2018). "I am tired of having to prove that my husband was dead." Dealing with practical matters in bereavement and the impact on the bereaved. *Death Studies, 42*(10), 627-635. https://doi.org/10.1080/07481187.2017.1415392

Boelen, P. A., &. Smid, G.E. (2017). The traumatic grief inventory self-report version (TGI-SR): Introduction and preliminary psychometric evaluation. *Journal of Loss and Trauma, 22*(3), 196-212. doi:10.1080/15325024.2017.1284488

Boss, P. (2012). Resilience as tolerance for ambiguity. In D. S. Becvar (Ed.), *Handbook of family resilience* (pp. 285-297). New York, NY: Springer.

Bottomley, J. S., Smigelsky, M. A., Bellet, B. W., Flynn, L., Price, J., & Neimeyer, R. A. (2019). Distinguishing the meaning making processes of survivors of suicide loss: An expansion of the meaning of loss codebook. *Death Studies, 43*(2), 92-102. doi:10.1080/07481187.2018.1456011

Bowlby, J. (1980). *Attachment and Loss: Loss, sadness, and depression* (Vol. 3). New York, NY: Basic Books.

Bowlby, J., & Parkes, C. M. (1970). Separation and loss within the family. In E. J. Anthony & C. Koupernik (Eds.), *The child in his family: Children at psychiatric risk* (pp. 197-216). Hoboken, NJ: John Wiley & Sons.

Boyraz, G., Horne, S. G., & Waits, J. B. (2015). Accepting death as part of life: Meaning in life as a means for dealing with loss among bereaved individuals. *Death Studies, 39*(1), 1-11.

Braam, A. W. (2017). Towards a multidisciplinary guideline religiousness, spirituality, and psychiatry: what do we need? *Mental Health, Religion & Culture, 20*(6), 579-588. doi:10.1080/13674676.2017.1377949

Cain, A. C., & LaFreniere, L. S. (2015). The Taunting of parentally bereaved children: An exploratory study. *Death Studies, 39*(4), 219-225. https://doi.org/10.1080/07481187.2014.975870

Campbell, (n.d). Suicide: finding hope, LOSS teams. http://www.suicidefindinghope.com/content/loss_teams

Cantwell-Bartel, A. (2018). The grief and coping of parents whose child has a constant life-threatening disability, hypoplastic left heart syndrome with reference to the dual process model. *Death Studies, 43*(9), 569-578. https://doi.org/10.1080/07481187.2017.1407380

Centers for Disease Control and Prevention (2018). *Vital Signs.* https://www.cdc.gov/vitalsigns/suicide/infographic.html

Cerel, J., Brown, M. M., Maple, M., Singleton, M., Van De Venne, J., Moore, M., & Flaherty, C. (2019). How many people are exposed to suicide? Not six. *Suicide and Life-Threatening Behavior, 49*(2), 529-534. doi:10.1111/sltb.12450

Cerel, J., McIntosh, J. L., Neimeyer, R. A., Maple, M., & Marshall, D. (2014). The continuum of survivorship: Definitional issues in the aftermath of suicide. *Suicide and Life-Threatening Behavior, 44,* 591–600. doi:10.1111/sltb.12093

Cerel, J., Padgett, J. H., Conwell, Y., Reed, G. A. (2009). A call for research: The need to better understand the impact of support groups for suicide survivors. *Suicide and Life-Threatening Behavior, 39*(3), 269–281.

Chopik, W. J. (2017). Death across the lifespan: Age differences in death-related thoughts and anxiety. *Death Studies, 41*(2), 69-77. https://doi.org/10.1080/07481 187.2016.1206997

Crosby, A. E., Ortega, L., & Melanson, C. (2011). Self-directed violence surveillance: Uniform definitions and recommended data elements, version 1.0. Atlanta (GA): Centers for Disease Control and Prevention, National Center for Injury Prevention and Control. https://www.cdc.gov/violenceprevention/pdf/Self-Directed-Violence-a.pdf

Dahdah, D. F., Rego, F., Vitale, R. H., Joaquim, T., Bombarda, T. B., & Nunes, R. (2018). Daily life and maternal mourning: A pilot study. *Death Studies.* doi: 10.1080/07481187.2018.1458762

Delespaux, E., and Zech, E. (2015). Why do bereaved partners experience interfering rumination? Evidence for deficits in cognitive inhibition, *Death Studies, 49*(8), 463-472. https://doi.org/10.1080/07481187.2014.958631

Doka, K. (Ed.). (2002). *Disenfranchised grief: New directions, challenges, and strategies for practice.* Champaign, IL: Research Press.

Doka, K. (2017). Complicated grief is complicated: Grief in the DSM-5. *Psychology Today.* https://www.psychologytoday.com/blog/good-mourning/201701/complicated-grief-is-complicated

Dougy Center. (n.d.). *Developmental grief responses.* http://www.dougy.org/grief-resources/developmental-grief-responses/

Dougy Center. (2017). *Developmental responses to grief.* https://www.dougy.org/docs/Developmental_Responses_2017.pdf

Eisma, M. C., & Stroebe, M.S. (2017). Rumination following bereavement: An overview. *Bereavement Care, 36*(2), 58-64. doi:10.1080/02682621.2017.1349291

Farberow, N. L. (2005). The mental health professional as suicide survivor. *Clinical Neuropsychiatry: Journal of Treatment Evaluation, 2*(1), 13-20. doi:2005-11020-003

Feigelman, W., Rosen, Z., Joiner, T., Silva, C., & Mueller, A. S. (2017). Examining longer-term effects of parental death in adolescents and young adults: Evidence from the national longitudinal survey of adolescent to adult health. *Death Studies, 41*(3), 133-143. https://doi.org/10.1080/07481187.2016.1226990

Finlayson, M., & Simmonds, J. G. (2018). Impact of client suicide on psychologists in Australia. *Australian Psychologist, 53*(1), 23-32. https://doi.org/10.1111/ap.12240

Finlayson, M., & Simmonds, J. (2019). Workplace Responses and Psychologists' Needs Following Client Suicide. *OMEGA – Journal of Death and Dying, 79*(1). 18-33. https://doi.org/10.1177/0030222817709693

Flahault, C., Dolbeault, S., Sankey, C., & Fasse, L. (2018). Understanding grief in children who have lost a parent with cancer: How do they give meaning to this experience? Results of an interpretative phenomenological analysis. *Death Studies, 42*(8), 483-490. doi:10.1080/07481187.2017.1383951

Fleming, K., & Drake, M. E. (2018). Theravive. *Persistent complex bereavement disorder DSM-5.* https://www.theravive.com/therapedia/persistent-complex-bereavement-disorder-dsm--5

Frankl, V. E. (1984). *Man's search for meaning: Revised and updated.* New York: Washington Square Press.

Freud, S. (1957). Mourning and melancholia. In J. Strachey (Ed. and Trans.), *The standard edition of the complete psychological works of Sigmund Freud* (Vol. 14), (pp. 243-258). London, England: Hogarth Press. (Original work published 1917).

Genest, C., Moore, M., & Nowicke, C. M. (2017). Posttraumatic growth after suicide. In K. Andriessen, K. Krysinska, & O. T. Grad (Eds.), *Postvention in action: The international handbook of suicide bereavement support* (pp. 50-59). Boston, MA: Hogrefe.

Goetter, E., Bui, E., Horenstein, A., Baker, A. W., Hoeppner, S., Charney, M., & Simon, N. M. (2018). The five-factor model in bereaved adults with and without complicated grief. *Death Studies, 1*(17). doi:10.1080/07481187.2018.1446059

Greene, N., & McGovern, K. (2017). Gratitude, psychological well-being, and perceptions of posttraumatic growth in adults who lost a parent in childhood. *Death Studies, 41*(7), 436-446. doi:10.1080/07481187.2017.1296505

Hagström, A. S. (2019). "Why did he choose to die?": A meaning-searching approach to parental suicide bereavement in youth. *Death Studies, 43*(2), 113-121. doi:10.1080/07481187.2018.1457604

Horowitz, M. J., Siegel, B., Holen, A., Bonanno, G. A., Milbrath, C., & Stinson, C. H. (1997). Diagnostic criteria for complicated grief disorder. *American Journal of Psychiatry, 154*(7), 904-910.

Jack, S.P., Petrosky E., Lyons, B. H., et al. Surveillance for Violent Deaths—National Violent Death Reporting System, 27 States, 2015. MMWR Surveillance Summary 2018 (67), No. SS-11, 1–32. doi:http://dx.doi.org/10.15585/mmwr.ss6711a1

Jordan, J. R. (2001). Is suicide bereavement different? A Reassessment of the Literature. *Suicide and Life-Threatening Behavior, 31*(1), 91–102.

Jordan, A. H., & Litz, B. T. (2014). Prolonged grief disorder: Diagnostic, assessment, and treatment considerations. *Professional Psychology: Research and Practice 45*(3), 180-187. http://dx.doi.org /10.1037/a0036836

Jordan, J. R., & McIntosh, J. L. (Eds.). (2011). *Grief after suicide: Understanding the consequences and caring for the survivors.* New York, NY: Routledge.

Joyce, M. (n.d.). Paradise Lost: When clients commit suicide. http://www.psychotherapy.net/article/client-suicide-article

Kaschka, W. P., & Rujescu, D. (2015). Biological aspects of suicidal behavior, 30. doi:https://www.karger.com/Article/PDF/439295

Kastenbaum, R. J. (2012). *Death, society, and human experience* (11th ed.) Upper Saddle River, NJ: Pearson.

Kawashima, D., & Kawano, K. (2016). Meaning reconstruction process after suicide: Life-story of a Japanese woman who lost her son to suicide. *OMEGA – Journal of Death and Dying, 75*(4), 360-375. https://doi.org/10.1177/0030222816652805

Klass, D., Silverman, P. R., & Nickman, S. L. (Eds.). (1996). *Continuing bonds: New understandings of grief.* Washington, DC: Taylor and Francis.

Klass, D., & Steffen, M. (Eds.). (2018). *Continuing bonds in bereavement: New directions for research and practice.* New York, NY: Routledge.

Kubler-Ross, E. (1969). *On death and dying.* NY: McMillan.

Lee, S. A. (2015). The Persistent Complex Bereavement Inventory: A measure based on the DSM-5. *Death Studies 39*(7), 399-410. doi:10.1080/07481187.2015.1029144

Lindemann, E. (1944). Symptomatology and management of acute grief. *American Journal of Psychiatry, 101,* 141-148.

Logan, E. L., Thornton, J. A., Kane, R. T., & Breen, L. J. (2018). Social support following bereavement: The role of beliefs, expectations, and support intentions. *Death Studies, 42*(8), 471-482. https://doi.org/10.1080/07481187.2017.1382610

Lumb, A. B., Beaudry, M., & Blanchard, C. (2017). Posttraumatic growth and bereavement. *OMEGA – Journal of Death and Dying, 75*(4), 311-336. https://doi.org/10.1177/0030222816652971

Lytje, M. (2017). Towards a model of loss navigation in adolescence. *Death Studies, 41*(5), 291-302. https://doi.org/10.1080/07481187.2016.1276488

Lytje, M. (2018). Voices that want to be heard: Using bereaved Danish students suggestions to update school bereavement response plans. *Death Studies, 42*(4), 254-267. doi:10.1080/07481187.2017.1346726

Maciejewski, P., & Prigerson, H. (2017). Prolonged, but not complicated, grief is a mental disorder. *The British Journal of Psychiatry, 211*, 1–2. https://www.researchgate.net/publication/320187553_Prolonged_but_not_complicated_grief_is_a_mental_disorder

Martin, T. L., & Doka, K. J. (2000). *Men don't cry, women do: Transcending gender stereotypes of grief.* Philadelphia, PA: Brunner/Mazel.

McManus, R., Walter, T., & Claridge, L. (2018). Restoration and loss after disaster: Applying the dual-process model of coping in bereavement. *Death Studies, 42*(7), 405-414. https://doi.org/10.1080/07481187.2017.1366599

McNiel, A., & Gabbay, P. (2018). *Understanding and supporting bereaved children: A practical guide for professionals.* NY: Springer Publishing.

Meagher, D. K., and Balk, D. E. (2013). *Handbook of Thanatology: The essential body of knowledge of death, dying, and bereavement* (2nd ed.). NY: Routledge.

Milic, J., Muka, T., Ikram, M. A., Franco, O. H., & Tiemeier, H. (2017). Determinants and predictors of grief severity and persistence: The Rotterdam Study. *Journal of Aging and Health, 29*(8), 1288-1307. https://doi.org/10.1177/0898264317720715

Millman, E., Neimeyer, R. A., & Gillies, J. (2016). Meaning of loss codebook (MLC). In R. A. Neimeyer (Ed.), *Techniques of grief therapy: Assessment and intervention* (pp. 51-58). New York, NY: Routledge.

Mowll, J., Lobb, E. A., & Wearing, M. (2016). The transformative meanings of viewing or not viewing the body after sudden death. *Death Studies, 40*(1), 46-53. https://doi.org/10.1080/07481187.2015.1059385

Murrell, A. R., Prigerson, H., & Jacobs, S. (2001). Traumatic grief as a distinct disorder: A rationale, consensus criteria, and a preliminary empirical test. In M. S. Stroebe, R. O. Hansson, W. Stroebe, and H. Schut, (Eds.), *Handbook of bereavement research: consequences, coping, and care.* Washington, DC: American Psychological Association, 613-645. doi:10.1037/10436-026

National Action Alliance for Suicide Prevention (2015). *Responding to grief, trauma, and distress after a suicide: U.S. national guidelines.* The Survivors of Suicide Loss Task Force of the National Action Alliance for Suicide Prevention. https://www.sprc.org/sites/default/files/migrate/library/RespondingAfter SuicideNationalGuidelines.pdf

Neimeyer, R. A. (2000). Searching for the meaning of meaning: Grief therapy and the process of reconstruction. *Death Studies, 24,* 541-558.

Neimeyer, R. A., (Ed.). (2001). *Meaning reconstruction and the experience of loss.* Washington, DC: American Psychological Association.

Neimeyer, R. A. (Ed.). (2012). *Techniques of grief therapy: Creative practices for counseling the bereaved.* New York: Routledge.

Neimeyer, R.A. (2019). Meaning reconstruction in bereavement: Development of a research program. *Death Studies, 43*(2), 79-91. doi:10.1080/07481187.2018. 1456620

Neimeyer, R. A., Cerel, J., & Maple, M. (2017). Recommendations for research on suicide loss: A commentary. *Death Studies, 41*(10), 673–679. doi:10.1080/07481 187.2017.1335555

Nwiran, Y., & Pennock, S. F. (2017). *Resilience in positive psychology. Bouncing back and going strong.* https://positivepsychologyprogram.com/resilience-in-positive-psychology/

Pearlman, L., Wortman, C., Feuer, C., Farber, C., & Rando, T. (2014). Treating traumatic bereavement: A practitioner's guide. New York: Guilford Press.

Pitman, A., Osborn, D., King, M., & Erlangsen, A. (2014). Effects of suicide bereavement on mental health and suicide risk. *The Lancet Psychiatry, 1*(1), 86–94. doi:10.1016/S2215-0366(14)70224X

Plakun, E. M., & Tillman, J. G. (2005). Responding to clinicians after loss of a patient to suicide. *Directions in Psychiatry, 25*(26), 301-308.

Prigerson, H. G., Horowitz, M. J., Jacobs, S. C., Parkes, C. M., Aslan, M., Goodkin, K., … Maciejewski, P. K. (2009). Prolonged grief disorder: Psychometric validation of criteria proposed for *DSM-V* and *ICD-11*. *PLOS Medicine, 6*(8), e1000121. doi:10.1371/journal.pmed.1000121

Prigerson, H., & Jacobs, S. (2001). Traumatic grief as a distinct disorder: A rationale, consensus criteria, and a preliminary empirical test. In M. S. Stroebe, W. Stroebe, & R. O. Hansson (Eds.). *Handbook of bereavement research* (pp. 613-645). Washington, DC: American Psychological Association.

Pritchard, T. R., & Buckle, J. L. (2018). Meaning-making after partner suicide: A narrative exploration using the meaning of loss codebook. *Death Studies, 42*(1), 35–44. doi:10.1080/07481187.2017.1334007

Rando, T.A. (1993). Treatment of complicated mourning. Champaign, IL: Research Press.

Rando, T. A., Doka, K. J., Fleming, S., Franco, M. H., Lobb, E. A., Parkes, C. M., & Steele, R. (2012). A call to the field: Complicated grief in the *DSM-5*. *OMEGA– Journal of Death and Dying, 65*(4), 251-255.

Rheingold, A. A., & Williams, J. L. (2018). Module-based comprehensive approach for addressing heterogeneous mental health sequelae of violent loss survivors. *Death Studies, 42*(3), 164-171. https://doi.org/10.1080/07481187.2017.1370798

Rubel, B. (2019). *Grief, Loss, and Bereavement: Helping individuals cope.* (4th ed.). MA: Western Schools.

Rynearson, E. K. (2001). *Retelling violent death.* Philadelphia: Brunner-Routledge.

Scharer, J. L., & Hibberd, R. (2019). Meaning differentiates depression and grief among suicide survivors. *Death Studies*, 1-9. doi:10.1080/07481187.2019.1586791

Shear, M. K., Simon, N., Wall, M., Zisook, S., Neimeyer, R., Duan, N., Reynolds, C., Lebowitz, B., Sung, S., Ghesquiere, A., Gorscak, B., Clayton, P., Ito, M., Nakajima, S., Konishi, T., Melhem, N., Meert, K., Schiff, M., O'Connor, M-F., First, M., Sareen, J., Bolton, J., Skritskaya, N., Mancini, A.D., & Keshaviah, A. (2011). Complicated grief and related bereavement issues for DSM-5. *Depression and anxiety, 28*(2), 103-117. doi:10.1002/da.20780. http://www.ncbi.nlm.nih.gov/pmc/articles/PMC3075805/

Sherba, R. T., Linley, J. V., Coxe, K. A., & Gersper, B. E. (2019). Impact of client suicide on social workers and counselors. *Social Work in Mental Health, 17*(3), 279-301. doi:10.1080/15332985.2018.1550028

Shields, C., Russo, K., & Kavanagh, M. (2019). Angels of Courage: The experiences of mothers who have been bereaved by suicide. *OMEGA – Journal of Death and Dying, 80*(2), 175-201.

Shneidman, E. S. (1969). Prologue: Fifty-eight years. In E. Shneidman (Ed.), *On the nature of suicide,* 1-30, San Francisco, CA: Jossey-Bass.

Shneidman, E. S. (1993). *Suicide as Psychache: A clinical approach to self-destructive behavior.* Northvale, NJ: Jason Aronson Inc.

Shneidman, E. S. (1972). Foreword. In A. C. Cain (Ed.), *Survivors of suicide* (pp. ix–xi). Springfield, IL: Charles C. Thomas.

Shneidman, E. S. (2004). *Autopsy of a suicidal mind.* New York, NY: Oxford University Press.

Sofka, C. J., Gilbert, K. R., & Noppe Cupit, I. (2012). *Dying, death, and grief in an online universe.* New York, NY: Springer Publishing Company.

Spatuzzi, R., Velia Giulietti, M., Ricciuti, M., Merico, F., Meloni, C., Fabbietti, P., Ottaviani, M., Violani, C., & Vespa, A. (2017). Quality of life and burden in family caregivers of patients with advanced cancer in active treatment settings and hospice care: A comparative study. *Death Studies, 41*(5), 276-283. https://doi.org/10.1080/07481187.2016.1273277

Speece, M. W., & Brent, S. B. (2014). Children's understanding of death: A review of three components of a death concept. *Child Development, 55*(5), 1671-1686.

Stanford School of Medicine, Palliative Care: Where do Americans die? https://palliative.stanford.edu/home-hospice-home-care-of-the-dying-patient/where-do-americans-die/

Stanton Chapple, H., Bouton, B. L., Man Chow, A. Y., Gilbert, K. R., Kosminsky, P., Moore J., & Whiting, P. P. (2017). The body of knowledge in thanatology: An outline. *Death Studies 41*(2), 118-125. https://doi.org/10.1080/07481187.2016.1231000

Stene-Larsen, K., & Reneflot, A. (2017). Contact with primary and mental health care prior to suicide: A systematic review of the literature from 2000 to 2017. *Scandinavian Journal of Public Health,* 1-9.

Stone, D. M., Luo, F., Lippy, C., & McIntosh, W. L. (2015). The role of social connectedness and sexual orientation in the prevention of youth suicide ideation and attempts among sexually active adolescents. *Suicide and Life-Threatening Behavior, 45*(4), 415-430.

Stroebe, M. S., & Schut, H. (2010). The dual process model of coping with bereave-ment: A decade on. *OMEGA – Journal of Death and Dying, 61*(4), 273-289. http://doi.org/10.2190/OM.61.4.b

Stylianou, P., & Zembylas, M. (2018). Peer support for bereaved children: Setting eyes on children's views through an educational action research project. *Death Studies, 42*(7), 446-455. doi:10.1080/07481187.2017.1369472

Tal, I., Mauro, C., Reynolds, III, C. F., Shear, K. M. Simon, N., Lebowitz, B., Skritskaya, N., Wang, Y., Qiu, X., Iglewicz, A., Glorioso, D., Avanzino, J., Loebach Wetherell, J., Karp, J. F., Robinaugh, D., & Zisook, S. (2017). Complicated grief after suicide bereavement and other causes of death. *Death Studies, 41*(5), 267-275. https://doi.org/10.1080/07481187.2016.1265028

Tedeschi, R. G., & Calhoun, L. G. (2004). Posttraumatic growth: Conceptual foundations and empirical evidence. *Psychological Inquiry, 15*(1), 1-18.

Tedeschi, R.G., & Calhoun, L.G. (2012). *Posttraumatic growth in clinical practice.* NY: Routledge.

Thompson, N., & Doka, K. (2017). Disenfranchised Grief. In N. Thompson & G.R. Cox (Eds.), *Handbook of the sociology of death, grief, and bereavement: A guide to theory and practice.* NY: Rutledge.

Thurman, T. R., Taylor, T. M., Luckett, B., Spyrelis, A., & Nice, J. (2018). Complicated grief and caregiving correlates among bereaved adolescent girls in South Africa. *Journal of Adolescence, 62*, 82-86. doi:https://doi.org/10.1016/j.adolescence.2017.11.009

Ting, L., Sanders, S., Jacobson, J. M., Power, J. R. (2006). Dealing with the Aftermath: A qualitative analysis of mental health social workers' reactions after a client suicide. *Social Work, 51*(4), 329–341. https://doi.org/10.1093/sw/51.4.329

University of Minnesota. (n.d.). *What is culture?* Center for Advanced Research on Language Acquisition. http://carla.umn.edu/culture/definitions.html

University of North Carolina at Charlotte. (n.d.). *What is PTG?* https://ptgi.uncc.edu/what-is-ptg/

Ursano, R. J., & Stein, M. B. (2017). The Army Study to Assess Risk and Resilience in Service members (Army STARRS) and The Study to Assess Risk and Resilience in Service members – Longitudinal Study (STARRS-LS). 2009–2020. *Center for the Study of Traumatic Stress 1*(15), 1-35.

US Department of Health and Human Services. (2001). *National strategy for suicide prevention: Goals and objectives for action.* Rockville, MD. Author.

Williams, J. L., & Rheingold, A. A. (2018). Introduction to the special section: Creative applications of restorative retelling. *Death Studies, 42*(1), 1-3. https://doi.org/ 10.1080/07481187.2017.1370415

Worden, W. (2018). *Grief counseling and grief therapy* (5th ed.). New York, NY: Springer.

World Health Organization. (2014). *Preventing suicide: A global imperative.* Geneva. Switzerland: Author. 1-89. https://www.who.int/mental_health/suicide-prevention/world_report_2014/en/

Yang, S., & Park, S. (2017). A Sociocultural Approach to Children's Perceptions of Death and Loss. *OMEGA – Journal of Death and Dying, 76*(1), 53-77. https://doi.org/10.1177/0030222817693138

Resources

After a Suicide: A Toolkit for Schools (2nd ed.): *https://afsp.org/our-work/education/after-a-suicide-a-toolkit-for-schools/*

After a Suicide: A Postvention Primer for Providers: *lifegard.tripod.com/After_a_Suicide.pdf*

After a Suicide: Religious Services: *https://theactionalliance.org/faith-hope-life/after-suicide-recommendations-religious-services-and-other-public-memorial-observances*

A Guide for Medical Examiners and Coroners: Best Practices for Talking with Families About Suicide *https://docs.wixstatic.com/ugd/a0415f_3160611bae3f4be69c8e86b1ec7ed4ce.pdf*

Alex Blackwood Foundation for Hope (Camp Alex): *alexblackwood.com*

Alliance of Hope for Suicide Loss Survivors: *allianceofhope.org*

American Academy of Bereavement: *thebereavementacademy.com*

American Association of Suicidology (AAS): *suicidology.org*

AAS-Helping Survivors of Suicide: What Can You Do? *https://www.preventionlane.org/wp-content/uploads/2016/10/Hepling-Survivors-of-Suicide_What-Can-You-Do.pdf*

American Foundation for Suicide Prevention (AFSP): *afsp.org*

AFSP-Children, Teens and Suicide Loss: *https://afsp.org/wp-content/flipbooks/childrenteenssuicideloss/?page=1*

AFSP-Healing Conversations: Personal Support for Survivors of Suicide Loss: *afsp.org/find-support/ive-lost-someone/healing-conversations/*

Association for Death Education and Counseling (ADEC): The Thanatology Association: *adec.org*

Befrienders Worldwide: *befrienders.org/*

Best Practices for Talking About Suicide for Medical Examiners and Coroners: *https://www.mecrecs.org/*

Beyond Blue: *https://www.beyondblue.org.au/the-facts/suicide-prevention/ understanding-suicide-and-grief/supporting-a-loved-one-after-they-have-lost- someone-to-suicide*

Breaking the Silence in the Workplace: *http://www.sprc.org/resources-programs/ breaking-silence-workplace-guide-employers-responding-suicide-workplace*

California Institute for Behavioral Health Solutions: After Rural Suicide: A Guide for Coordinated Community Postvention Response: *https://www.cibhs.org/sites/ main/files/file-attachments/after_rural_suicide_guide_2016rev.pdf*

Camp Kita: Children's Bereavement Camp for Suicide Loss Survivors: *https:// campkita.com/*

Carson J. Spencer Foundation: *carsonjspencer.org*

The Catholic Charities: Loving Outreach to Survivors of Suicide: *https://www. catholiccharities.net/GetHelp/OurServices/Counseling/Loss.aspx*

The Center for Complicated Grief: *https://complicatedgrief.columbia.edu/ professionals/complicated-grief professionals/overview/*

Center for Grief and Loss: *griefloss.org/*

Center for Suicide Awareness: *https://www.centerforsuicideawareness.org/*

Centering Corporation: *centering.org/*

Clinicians as Survivors: After a Suicide Loss: */pages.iu.edu/~jmcintos/basicinfo.htm*

Comfort Zone Camp: *https://www.comfortzonecamp.org/*

Compassion Books: *www.compassionbooks.com*

Compassionate Friends: Surviving Your Child's Suicide: *https://www.compassion-atefriends.org/surviving-childs-suicide/*

Cope Foundation: *copefoundation.org/*

Davenee Foundation: *daveneefoundation.org/*

Digital Memorial Quilts: *afsp.org/find-support/ive-lost-someone/digital-memory-quilt/create-a-new-quilt-square/*

The Dougy Center: National Center for Grieving Children and Families: *dougy.org/*

Emma's Place of Staten Island: *www.emmasplacesi.com/*

Find a Suicide Loss Survivors Support Group: *afsp.org/find-support/ive-lost- some-one/find-a-support-group/*

Friends for Survival: Offering Help After a Suicide Death: *friendsforsurvival.org/*

The Gift of Second: *http://thegiftofsecond.com/*

The Glendon Association: *glendon.org/*

Heartbeat: *https://www.heartbeatsurvivorsaftersuicide.org/*

Help at Hand: A Guide for Funeral Directors: *http://www.sprc.org/sites/default/files/migrate/library/funeraldirectors.pdf*

Hope Squad: *hopesquad.com/postvention/*

How to Talk to Kids About Suicide: *https://drrobynsilverman.com/how-to-talk-to-kids-about-suicide-with-dr-dan-reidenberg/*

International Association for Suicide Prevention (IASP): *info/postvention.php*

International Society for Traumatic Stress Studies: *ISTSS.org*

The Jason Foundation: *www.jasonfoundation.com*

The JED Foundation: *jedfoundation.org/*

The Joseph T. Quinlan Bereavement Center: *copewithgrief.org*

Kara: *kara-grief.org/support-for/adults/*

Lifesavers Blog-AFSP: *https://afsp.org/lifesaver-blog/*

LOSS Team: *lossteam.com/*

A Manager's Guide to Suicide Postvention in the Workplace: *https://idph.iowa.gov/Portals/1/Files/SubstanceAbuse/managers_postvention.pdf*

Mental Health America: *mentalhealthamerica.net/*

Moyer Foundation (Camp Erin): *moyerfoundation.org*

National Alliance for Grieving Children: *childrengrieve.org/*

National Alliance on Mental Illness: *nami.org/*

National Child Traumatic Stress Network (NCTSN): *nctsn.org/what-is-child-trauma/trauma-types/traumatic-grief*

NASPA Student Affairs Administrators in Higher Education, Postvention: A guide for response to suicide on college campuses. *https://www.naspa.org/focus-areas/mental-health/postvention-a-guide-for-response-to-suicide-on-college-campuses*

National Organization for Victim Assistance: *trynova.org*

National Center for Victims of Crime: *victimsofcrime.org/*

National Suicide Prevention Lifeline, 24/7, Free and Confidential Support: 1-800-273-TALK (8255); for Hard of Hearing 1-800-799-4889; en Español 1-888-628-9454. *suicidepreventionlifeline.org/*

National Suicide Prevention Lifeline: Lifeline Online Postvention Manual *http:// www.sprc.org/sites/default/files/migrate/library/LifelineOnlinePostventionManual.pdf*

Open to Hope: *opentohope.com/*

Our Side of Suicide: *http://www.oursideofsuicide.com/*

Parents of Suicides/Friends & Families of Suicides: *pos-ffos.com/*

Pastoral Postvention: *https://theactionalliance.org/sites/default/files/fhl_competencies_ v8_interactive.pdf*

Posttraumatic Growth Research Group: *ptgi.uncc.edu/*

The Public Health Approach to Prevention *sprc.org/sites/sprc.org/files/library/phasp.pdf*

QPR Institute for Suicide Prevention: *courses.qprinstitute.com/*

Reach Out.com: ie.reachout.com/loss-and-grief/supporting-a-friend-after-someone-dies-from-suicide/

Riverside Trauma Center: *http://traumacenter.wpengine.com/wp-content/uploads/ 2015/03/Postventionguidelines.pdf*

SAFE-T Pocket Guides for Clinicians: *store.samhsa.gov/product/Suicide-Assessment-Five-Step-Evaluation-and-Triage-SAFE-T-Pocket-Card-for-Clinicians/SMA09-4432*

The Samaritans: *https://www.samaritans.org/* NYC: *samaritansnyc.org/* MA: *samaritanshope.org/*

Sibling Survivors of Suicide Loss: *siblingsurvivors.com/*

Substance Abuse and Mental Health Services Administration: *www.samhsa.gov/*

Suicide Attempt Survivors Task Force of the National Action Alliance for Suicide Prevention: *actionallianceforsuicideprevention.org/sites/actionallianceforsuicide-prevention.org/files/The-Way-Forward-Final-2014-07-01.pdf*

Suicide Awareness Voices of Education (SAVE): *save.org*

Suicide: Finding Hope: *suicidefindinghope.com/*

Suicide Grief Support Forum: *suicidegrief.com/*

Suicide Prevention Resource Center (SPRC): *sprc.org*

SPRC Toolkit for Schools *http://www.sprc.org/resources-programs/after-suicide-toolkit-schools*

Suicide Safety Plan: *suicidesafetyplan.com*

Support After a Suicide: *supportaftersuicide.org.au/*

Surviving After a Suicide Loss Blog: *https://survivingafterasuicide.com/blog/*

Tragedy Assistance Program for Survivors (TAPS): *https://www.taps.org/ suicide-postvention*

Trauma Institute & Child Trauma Institute: *childtrauma.com/*

Trevor Project (LGBTQ): *thetrevorproject.org/*

United Suicide Survivors International: *https://unitesurvivors.org/*

Violent Death Bereavement Society: *vdbs.org/html/director.html*

Yellow Ribbon: *yellowribbon.org/*

Zero Suicide in Health and Behavioral Health Care Toolkit: *zerosuicide.sprc.org/ toolkit*

Additional Readings

American Association of Suicidology (2003). *SOS: A Handbook for Survivors of Suicide*

Anderson, R., & Phillips, L. (2016). *Suicide Survivors' Club: A Family's Journey Through the Death of Their Loved One*

Andriessen, K. Krysinska, K., & Grad, O. T. (2017). *Postvention in Action: The International Handbook of Suicide Bereavement Support*

Ashton, J. (2019). *Life After Suicide: Finding Courage, Comfort & Community After Unthinkable Loss*

Auerbach, S. (2017). *I'll Write Your Name on Every Beach: A Mother's Quest for Comfort, Courage and Clarity After Suicide Loss*

Barrett, T. W. (2013). *Life After Suicide: The Survivor's Grief Experience* (2nd ed.)

Baxter, D. (2014). *Surviving Suicide: Searching for "Normal" with Heartache & Humor*

Bolton, I., & Mitchell, C. (1983). *My Son . . . My Son . . .: A Guide to Healing After Death, Loss, or Suicide*

Bolton, I. (2019). *Voices of Healing and Hope: Conversations on Grief after Suicide*

Burgess, M. E. (2013). *Handbook of Hope: First Aid for Surviving the Suicide of a Loved One*

Cambria, A. (2017). *My New Normal: Surviving Suicide Loss*

Cammarata, D. T. (2009). *Someone I Love Died by Suicide: A Story for Child Survivors and Those Who Care for Them*

Cobain, B., & Larch, J. (2005). *Dying to Be Free: A Healing Guide for Families After a Suicide*

DeSousa, M. H. (2011). *The Forgotten Mourners: Sibling Survivors of Suicide*

The Dougy Center. (2011). *Understanding Suicide, Supporting Children*

Doucet, G. (2015). *Let Go and Let Love: Survivors of Suicide Loss Healing Handbook*

Fine, C. (1999). *No Time to Say Goodbye: Surviving the Suicide of a Loved One*

Glynn, M. (2016). *The Scattering of All: Tales from Extraordinary Survivors of Suicide Loss*

Hsu, A. Y. (2017). *Grieving a Suicide: A Loved One's Search for Comfort, Answers,* and Hope

Jordan, J., & Baugher, B. (2016). *After Suicide Loss: Coping with Your Grief,* (2nd ed.)

Jordan, J. R., & Mcintosh, J. L. (2015). *Grief After Suicide: Understanding the Consequences and Caring for the Survivors*

Kilburn, L. H. (2008). *Reaching Out after Suicide: What's Helpful and What's Not*

Kirk, A. R. (2009). *Black Suicide: The Tragic Reality of America's Deadliest Secret*

Klock Morel, J. (Ed.) (2013). *Beyond Surviving: A Compilation of Stories from Survivors of Suicide Loss*

Knapp, R. J., & Pincus, J. D. (2019). *Sons of Suicide: A Memoir of Friendship*

Landon, J. (2017). *Growing Through Grief: A Guide to Healthy Healing After Losing a Loved One to Suicide*

Lesoine, R., & Chophel, M. (2009). *Unfinished Conversation: Healing from Suicide and Loss*

Lidbeck, B. (2016). *The Gift of Second: Healing from the Impact of Suicide*

Linn-Gust, M. (2010). *Rocky Roads: The Journeys of Families Through Suicide Grief*

Lukas, C., & Seiden, H. M. (2007). *Silent Grief: Living in the Wake of Suicide*

Marcus, E. (2010). *Why Suicide? Questions and Answers About Suicide, Suicide Prevention, and Coping with the Suicide of Someone You Know*

Marshall, N. (2018). *Getting Through It: A Workbook for Suicide Survivors*

McAuliffe, R. J., and Jackel, P. (2019). *Wake Me from the Nightmare: Hope, Healing, and Empowerment After Suicide Loss*

Montgomery, S. S., & Coale, S. M. (2015). *Supporting Children After a Suicide Loss: A Guide for Parents and Caregivers*

Myers, M. F., & Fine, C. (2006). *Touched by Suicide: Hope and Healing After Loss*

Palrang, M., & McMahon, J. (2018). *Frantic Unleashed: Navigating Life After Suicide—A Survivor's Journal*

Redfield Jamison, K. (2000). *Night Falls Fast: Understanding Suicide*

Robinson, R. (2001). *Survivors of Suicide*

Rolheiser, R. (2017). *Bruised and Wounded: Struggling to Understand Suicide*

Saul, D. (2016). *Did You Know I Would Miss You? The Transformational Journey of the Suicide Survivor*

Savoie, L. (2014). *The Ripple Effect: Invisible Impact of Suicide*

Sexton-Jones, S. (2002). *When Someone You Love Completes Suicide*

Smolin, A., & Guinan, J. (1993). *Healing After the Suicide of a Loved One*

Tervo, R. (2017). *Shattered: From Grief to Joy After My Son's Suicide*

Walraven-Thissen, A. (2019). *Responding After Suicide: A Practical Guide to Immediate Postvention*

Wickersham, J. (2008). *The Suicide Index: Putting my Father's Death in Order*

Wolfelt, A. D. (2002). *The Wilderness of Suicide Grief: Finding Your Way*

Wolfelt, A. D. (2009). *Understanding Your Suicide Grief: Ten Essential Touchstones for Finding Hope and Healing Your Heart*

Wrobleski, A. (2002). *Suicide Survivors: A Guide for Those Left Behind*

About the Author

Three weeks prior to **Barbara Rubel** giving birth to triplets, her father died by suicide. Her story was featured in the Emmy award winning documentary, *Fatal Mistakes: Families Shattered by Suicide,* narrated by Mariette Hartley. Barbara is a champion for professional well-being and has pioneered a unique approach to addressing suicide postvention and vicarious trauma by bringing a deep understanding of thanatology and personal resilience to her work. She is a professional speaker and trainer for corporations, conferences, universities, and government agencies. She is a sought-after keynoter and seminar leader whose list of clients span more than 500 organizations.

With refreshing clarity and humor, Barbara's speaking engagements are designed to give audiences powerful and practical strategies that can be implemented immediately. She is a board-certified expert in traumatic stress, and a diplomate with the American Academy of Experts in Traumatic Stress. She received a bachelor of science degree in psychology and a master of arts degree in community health, with a concentration in thanatology, both from Brooklyn College. Audiences learn a practical method to better serve suicide loss survivors while focusing on their own self-care. As an author and speaker, Barbara guides you through the theory and the practice of her approach.

Barbara is the author of the 30-hour continuing education course book for nurses, *Loss, Grief, and Bereavement: Helping Individuals Cope* (4th ed.), sold through Western Schools. She is a contributing writer to *Thin Threads: Grief and Renewal; Open to Hope's Fresh Grief; Coaching for Results: Expert Advice from 25 Top International Coaches; Keys to a Good Life: Wisdom to Unlock Your Power Within;* and *Remembering Our Angels.* She has also authored numerous articles on coping with loss and building personal resilience.

Barbara created and facilitated Sharing Our Loss After Suicide (SOLAS), a grief support group for suicide loss survivors. She was a hospice bereavement coordinator, and served as an adjunct teacher at Brooklyn College where she taught undergraduate and masters-level courses in Death, Life and Health; Children and Death; Health Crisis Intervention; and Health Counseling. Barbara is a consultant with the U.S. Department of Justice, Office for Victims of Crime Training and Technical Assistance Center (OVCTTAC) and co-wrote its training.

Invite Barbara to Speak at Your Event

By phone: 732-422-0400

By E-mail: *BarbaraRubel@BarbaraRubel.com*

By Snail Mail: Griefwork Center, Inc.

PO Box 5177, Kendall Park, NJ 08824

Website: GriefWorkCenter.com